Start a Freelance Business Today

Freelancing with YouTube, WordPress, Upwork and Fiverr!

Jerry Banfield

Editor: Michel Gerard

Publisher: *https://jerrybanfield.com/books*

COPYRIGHT

Start a Freelance Business Today - Copyright © Jerry Banfield - 2016

More Books by Jerry Banfield

https://jerrybanfield.com/books

TABLE OF CONTENTS

PREFACE

Thank you very much for reading this book! You are reading this now because you want to learn more about freelancing online. I hope that I will answer all the questions you may have in the different chapters of this book and help you make the right choice for a strategy that will work for you to have success as a freelancer online.

VISIT
JERRYBANFIELD.COM

Get updates about Jerry Banfield's newest books and courses via email.

How did you get here with me?

In 2005 while I was in college at the *University of South Carolina*, I tried to start working online. I signed up for an *MLM* program and a survey website. A month later, I had refunds from both and figured working online was not possible because everything was a scam. The truth was I was afraid to fail again.

In 2011, I moved in with my wife and launched an online business focusing on video game addiction in an attempt to avoid dealing with any of my other problems. In a few months, I changed my business to selling T-shirts because I realized there was no money in video game addiction. A year after starting my business, I dropped out of my criminology *PHD* program at the *University of South Florida* to run my business full time, which by then had changed to helping clients with *Facebook* and *Google* ads based on my experience failing to do them successfully for myself.

In 2013, I started sharing everything I knew for free on *YouTube* because I hoped it would help me get more clients. By April 2014, I was nearly bankrupt after failing at *15+* different business models. I was also nearly dead from trying to drink the pain away and fortunately the fear of death motivated me to get into recovery. Being in recovery motivated me to focus more on being of true service to others and less on what I would get out of it. I started making courses online with *Udemy* which soon turned into my first real business. I partnered with as many talented instructors as I could and learned from top instructors how to get my courses the most sales.

In 2015, I tried making some inspirational videos sharing what I learned in recovery and got an amazing response on *YouTube*. To make the background on my videos more interesting, I started making the inspirational videos while playing video games. To make a more helpful website, I hired a freelancer to convert the videos into blog posts. A *Udemy* student named *Michel Gerard* then helped me turn those posts into books.

By 2016, the *Udemy* courses I was teaching had made nearly *2 million dollars* in sales with me receiving over *$600,000* of that. Things went so well on *Udemy* that they decided to launch a new pricing policy in April 2016 that reduced sales by *80%* site-wide which encouraged many instructors to leave. Since I did not take the hint, *Udemy* chose to ban me based on what they said were policy violations despite my best efforts to work within the rules.

Now I am trying out live streaming video games both for the self-help message and the hands on tutorials that I watch when I am playing a new game. Again I take another leap of faith in my business online which I hope is for the right reason of being in loving service here with you.

Thank you very much for reading this and I hope you enjoy the rest!

Jerry Banfield

CHAPTER 1

Building everything online around you will allow you to grow and change

In this first chapter we are going to explore together the different tools you can use as a freelancer to help you build your credibility and grow your business.

There is a good chance that what you are doing today is not the same that what you will do in the future.

What I do online keeps changing and where you can find me stays the same.

I will explain how to get the advantage over other freelancers and _show people what you can do on your YouTube channel._

WordPress is a content management system that can help you build a very professional website very easily. _What is WordPress and how am I using it?_

If you don't know where to look for freelance work online, start with _Upwork_, which is a global online work platform. _What is Upwork and how am I using it?_

Fiverr is similar to *Upwork,* but has a simple system starting at *$5* per job performed. *What is Fiverr and how am I using it?*

Finally, I will show you how *making social media and freelancing profiles that match your name* will help people find you when they search you on the Internet.

Read on…

What I do online keeps changing and where you can find me stays the same

What I do online keeps changing and where you can find me stays the same. That is why having a website with your own custom *URL* is so nice. If you look at my blog *(jerrybanfield.com/blog-posts/)*, you can see that there are tons of different subjects.

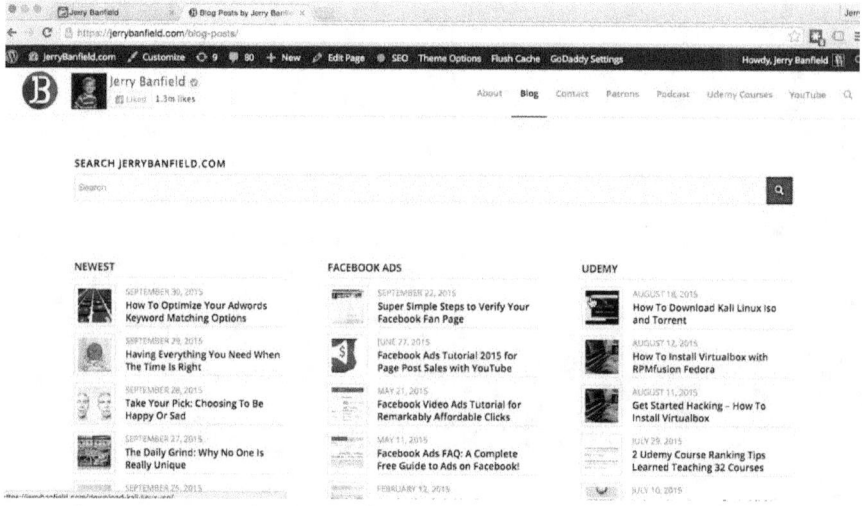

There is a category for *Facebook* ads, *Udemy*, *Patreon*, *Google*, *YouTube*, digital marketing, success online, business, dating and all kinds of relationships, even the beginning of new novels.

Jerry Banfield & Michel Gerard

What I do keeps changing and where you can find me stays the same. This is such a nice approach because then, no matter what you start doing, no matter what new ideas you have, you can put them all in the same place when you have a website.

No matter where you start, a *YouTube* channel, online courses *(jerrybanfield.com/shop/)* or podcasts, whatever it is, you can always link out from your website.

The website is the foundation of where the most enthusiastic people can find you. I always send people to my website because no matter what I'm doing, it is relevant.

I've made all kinds of changes on my website at *jerrybanfield.com*. When I started I didn't have any courses, so I showed off different things on it. In the future, if I do something different like the live streaming I am starting to do now, then I can feature that.

When you brand your site for a company, you make it on a certain theme, but you always will change over time, and then you run the risk of becoming irrelevant.

When you use your own name as the *URL*, people can

always just search and then find you on your website.

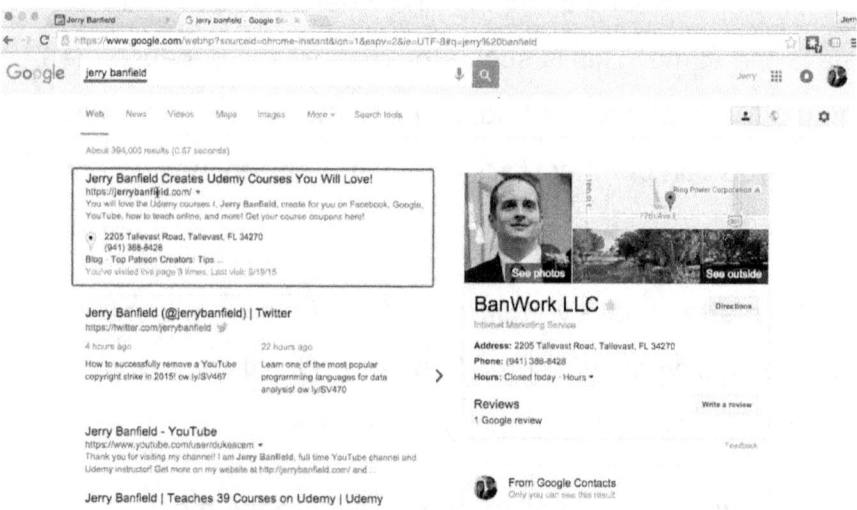

When people search my name online, they find my website.

When you set everything up like that, it's so much easier, especially if you change what you do all the time because you are not sure of what you want to do. Everything you do can collectively add up to an amazing result when you just put all of it on your website, particularly in the form of a blog.

If you go on my website, my blog is just a laundry list of all the things I do. I can just set it up to feature whatever I want to showcase most, right at the top. Then, all the other posts work to get traffic.

This is the easiest setup I found to work online, which is why I am sharing this with you.

Show people what you can do
on your *YouTube* channel

The trick to being a successful freelancer online is to show people what you can do.

Show them!

There are millions of freelancers online and almost everyone can talk a great game about what they would do. Almost every freelancer can talk to you about all of these things that they can do and sell you on them.

What very few freelancers can do is show you proof that they really can do something. For me the most challenging part with hiring freelancers is that everyone can talk and almost none can show proof.

That gives you the opportunity to get the advantage and show proof, and *YouTube* is the easiest way. There's nothing that's so effective at showing proof as a *YouTube* channel with videos of what you do. When you look at my *YouTube* channel at *www.youtube.com/c/JerryBanfield*, the videos show what I do.

Jerry Banfield & Michel Gerard

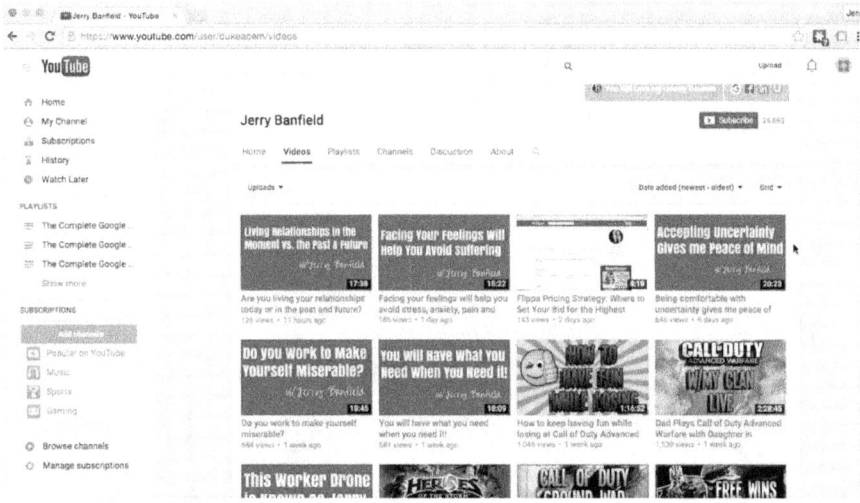

You can see the work I do, you can see the thumbnails and you can see that I'm doing things. In fact, you can see exactly what I'm doing.

My *YouTube* channel is where I show what I do and that more than likely is why you are reading this. Either you watched my *YouTube* channel first, or the sales that came from my *YouTube* channel got you here from some other method.

Putting videos on your *YouTube* channel and uploading them consistently is the easiest way to show people what you do, and it's a huge thing you can use to stand out. One of the most powerful things you can use are tutorial videos because if you are offering to do some work for someone, showing them how you do it yourself is incredibly helpful.

If I wanted to get *Google AdWords* clients, this is exactly what I'd use.

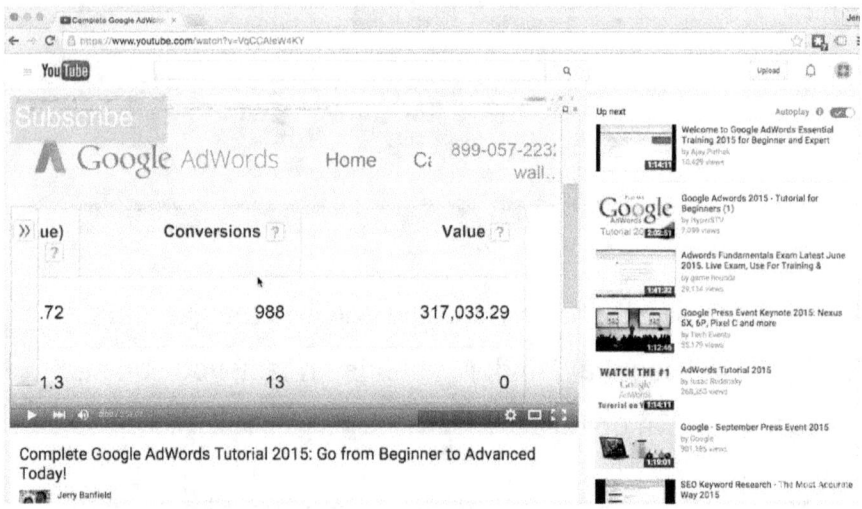

This is an almost *4* hour video showing me doing *Google AdWords*. It has specific time points and it has chapters.

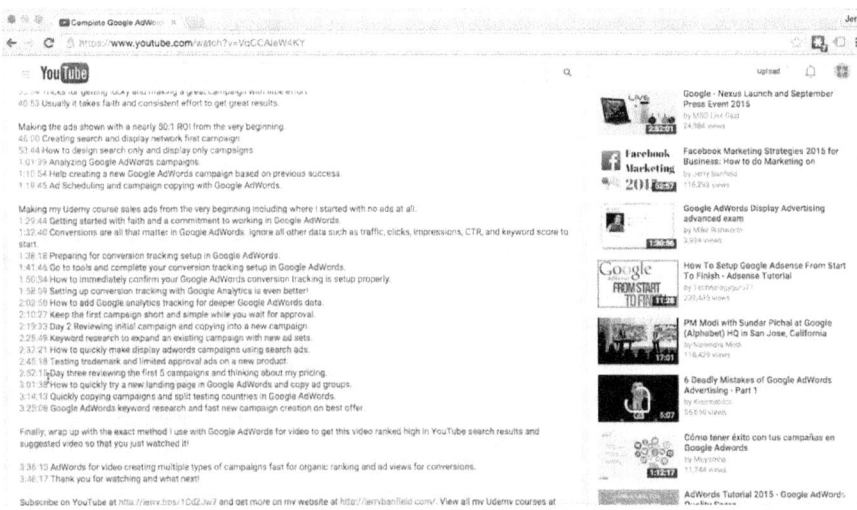

This is one of the top *Google AdWords* videos on *YouTube*. All you have to do is show what you can do in a video and then it's so much easier to get hired.

When you get to work on a *YouTube* channel, you can easily start showing what you do and you'll get so much better at what you are trying to do when you get to work on teaching it. If you look at my *YouTube* home below, what you'll see is these viral videos.

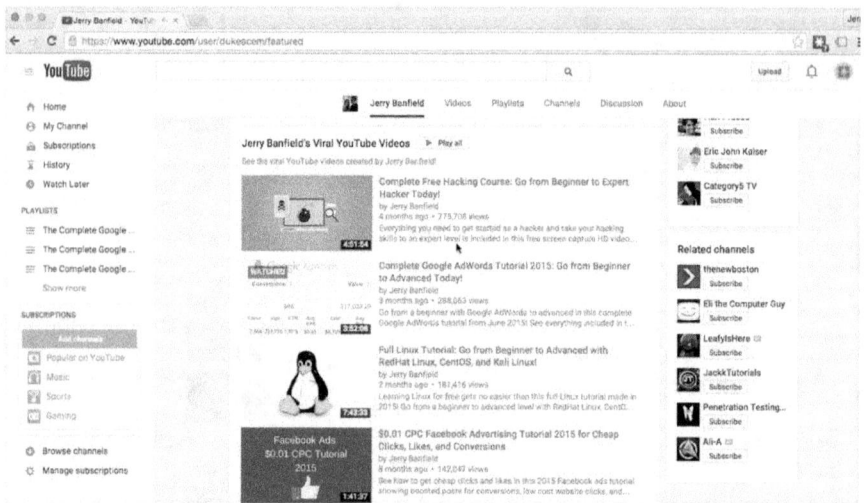

All of my best videos are teaching videos. The first is a hacking one, then *AdWords*, *Linux* and *Facebook*.

These are teaching videos and the more I teach, the better I had to get with what I'm doing. When you make videos showing what you are doing, then, you will learn it better and have proof that you can do it at the same time.

It's absolutely beautiful.

There's no system I am aware of that is more effective at both getting people to find you and showing what you can do to people who already have found you.

I love *YouTube*.

YouTube is the foundation of everything good that's

happened to me online. That's why I take you through and show you exactly what you can do to get your *YouTube* channel showing what you are doing, and use it to build whatever it is you're trying to do.

What is *WordPress* and how am I using it?

WordPress is a free and open source content management system.

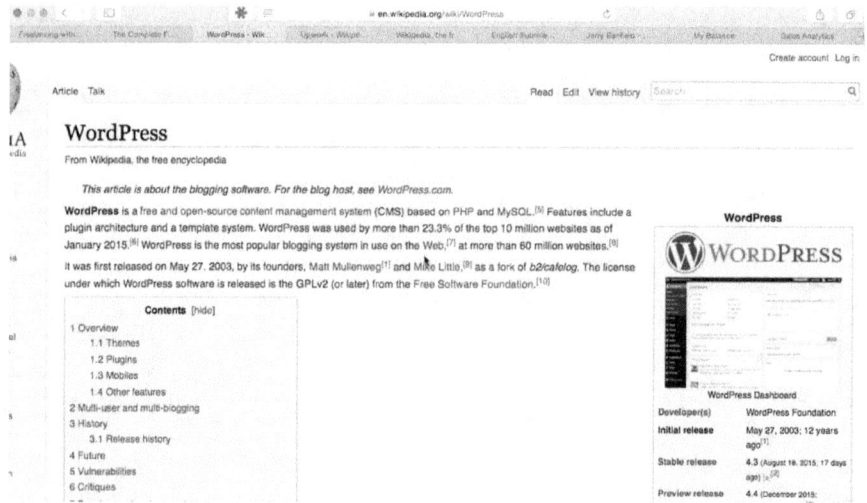

What does that mean?

That means *WordPress* is where you can create and get to work on your website and that's exactly what I'm doing with it today. *JerryBanfield.com* is created and managed in *WordPress*.

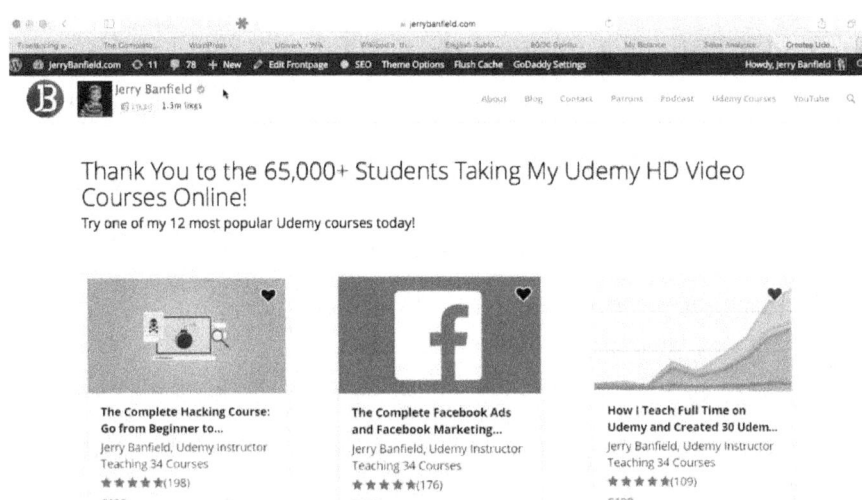

Below you can see how the *WordPress* dashboard looks like with all the settings and the backend.

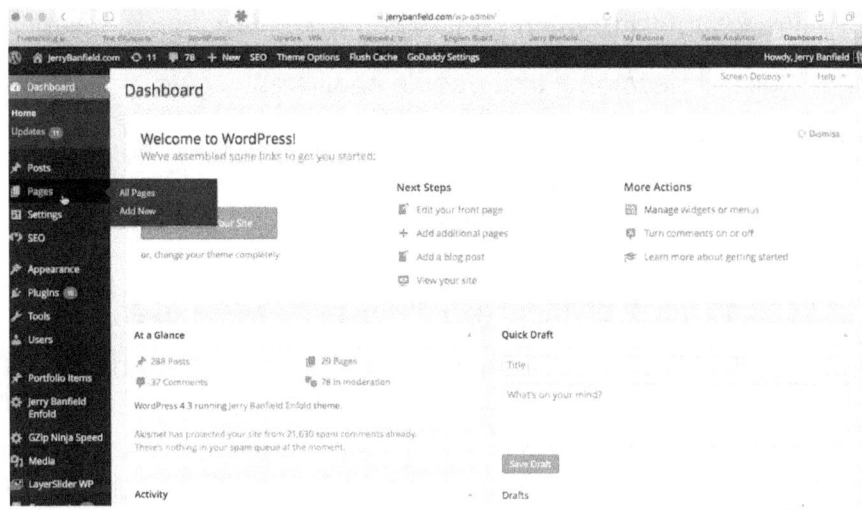

You can make blog posts or pages on it that are fixed,

instead of being a part of the blog. Then you have all the different settings you can do to make your website look and function the way you want it to.

WordPress is used by more than *23* percent of the top *10* million websites and it's the most popular blogging system in use on the web.

WordPress is the standard way that you make a website and add content to it. It's ridiculously easy to use and there are many different web hosting platforms that can give you cheap hosting for it. It's a simple way to make a professional website and you don't have to know anything about coding.

I know almost nothing about coding and I have a website that looks professional that people consistently give compliments on.

They say: *"Oh! This is a nice website."*

You can get everything right through my website and you can see that I put a lot of energy in it. This is my blog below.

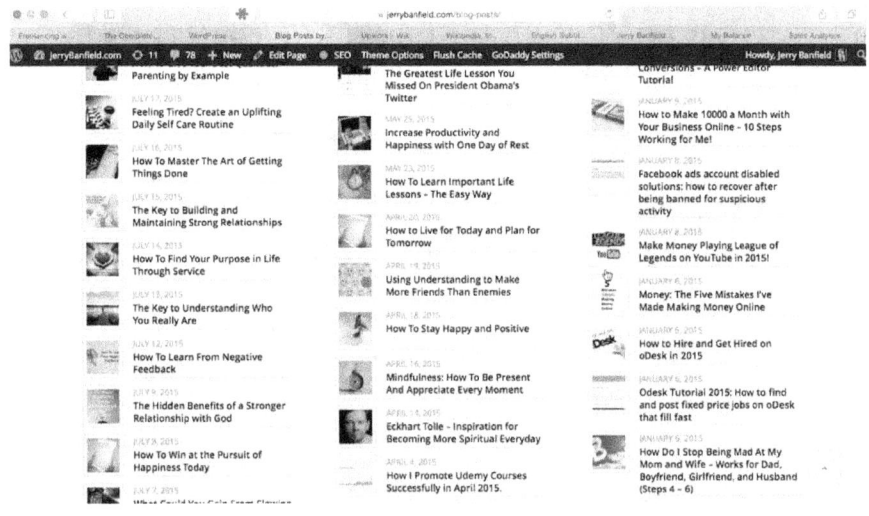

These are all blog posts and most of these are all fairly new. Now I have a system for doing this. The beauty of *WordPress* is that it's easy to get help with. Also, when you start having things go well, it is scalable. You can set up *WordPress* right on your own without having any prior experience.

WordPress is very helpful to freelancers online. Building a professional website is one of the most helpful things you can have to put yourself as an upscale freelancer. *WordPress* will help you get a lot more work.

What is *Upwork* and how am I using it?

Upwork, formerly known as *Odesk* or *Elance* is a global online work platform where businesses and independent professionals connect and collaborate remotely.

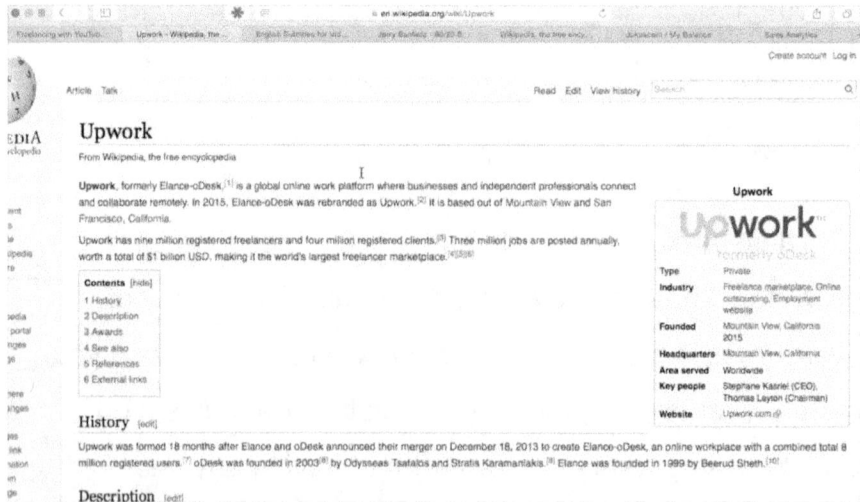

What does that mean? It means that *9* million registered freelancers and *4* million registered clients get together to post or work on jobs. *Upwork* is the largest global freelancer marketplace and here is what I'm doing.

Jerry Banfield & Michel Gerard

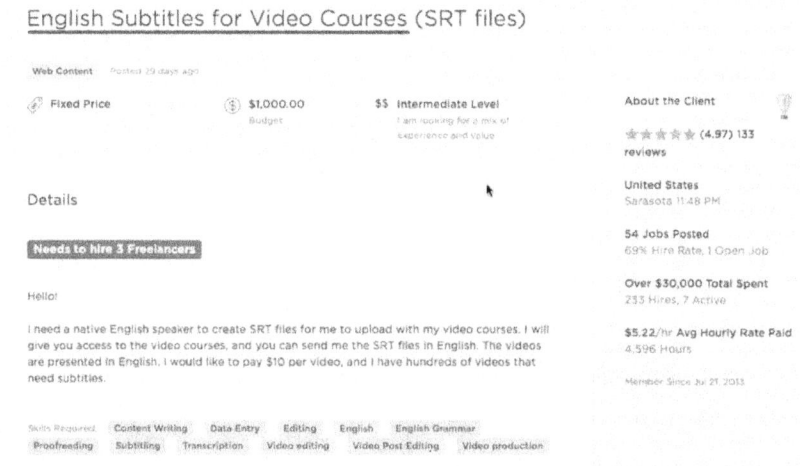

Today, I have a job posted: *"English Subtitles for Video Courses."* It is for my *Udemy* courses.

As you can see, I've hired a lot of people on *Upwork*.

> Platinum Tier: One of the top clients on Upwork

About the Client

⭐⭐⭐⭐⭐ (4.97) 133 reviews

United States
Sarasota 11:48 PM

54 Jobs Posted
69% Hire Rate, 1 Open Job

Over $30,000 Total Spent
233 Hires, 7 Active

Upwork is a number one place I've used to find new people to hire. I've spent over *30,000* dollars and I've hired *233* people on *Upwork* and when it was *Odesk*. I'm still using *Upwork* to find new freelancers, I have jobs open and I have consistently had a great experience.

A *"Platinum Tier"* client means that you are one of the top clients on *Upwork*. I pay a lot of people to help me with my business on this platform, so you can expect that it's possible for you to get paid on *Upwork* too.

I also have a freelancing profile on *Upwork,* but I've never actually got a job on it. However, what it did do is help me get to know myself better.

From doing my freelancing profile on *Upwork*, I realized I needed to learn more about how to present myself effectively online. When you get in with all the other freelancers on *Upwork*, you realize that you need to stand out somehow and you need to build resources like a website and a *YouTube* channel that show what you can do.

It's not good enough to simply make a profile and hope for

good results when you apply to jobs. You need to really show what you can do in order to stand out. So at least, I have an *Upwork* profile that tries to lead by example.

If you'll notice below, I've taken tests on *Upwork* and this helped me get to know what skills I had.

Tests

Name	Score (out of 5)		Time to Complete	
Internet Marketing Test	4.75	Top 10%	14 mins	Details
Analytical Skills Test	4.25	Top 10%	45 mins	Details
Google AdWords Test	4.15	Top 20%	21 mins	Details
Social Media Marketing Test	4.50	Top 10%	16 mins	Details
U.S. English Basic Skills Test	4.50	Top 10%	22 mins	Details

Even though I never actually got hired on *Upwork,* I never spent much time trying to get hired. I spent a lot of time going through and taking these tests to get this top ten percent scores.

I've got now *20%* for the *Google Adwords* test as apparently more people have taken the test since then. I got to know myself better through creating my *Upwork* profile.

I do a lot in terms of hiring people and I've taken the time to go make an *Upwork* profile. I showed you my blog in a previous section and this is how I've got help with all those blog posts.

I have a freelancer and she does a great job with it. She earns right now *$18* an hour and she is likely going to get more in the future when she continues to grow and build her profile up. I'll have to raise my rate to keep up.

She's earned over *$2,000* simply by transcribing videos into posts and then posting them on my *WordPress* website. She has a part time job and she can work up to *20* hours per week whenever she wants to, and she does something that is very useful for me.

That is the power of *Upwork*.

You could very easily, compared to a lot of other ways, find a job and earn *$20* an hour that you can do from the comfort of your home. You can very easily get yourself set up on *Upwork* and start earning *$20* an hour or so, by doing some work for about *20* hours per week.

If you want to go that route, you will be interested by chapter 7 where I'll give you more information on how you can use *Upwork* as a freelancer.

What is *Fiverr* and how am I using it?

Fiverr is similar to *Upwork* as it is a global online freelancing marketplace. The difference is that *Fiverr* has a simple system starting at *$5* per job performed. You use a specific task that you offer to do and then people come to buy that specific task from you.

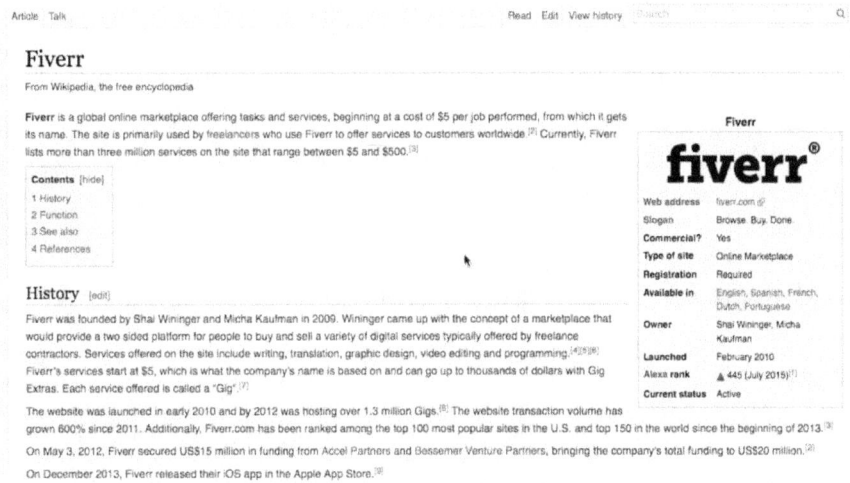

Fiverr is like a simplified version of *Upwork*.

Upwork can be very complicated in terms of getting your job, applying and finding a client, and *Fiverr* is kind of a simple version. I've used *Fiverr* to grow my business greatly, by buying gigs from people who offered things that I needed. I've spent over *$5,000* as a client on *Fiverr*, which is roughly equivalent to *1,000* gigs ordered.

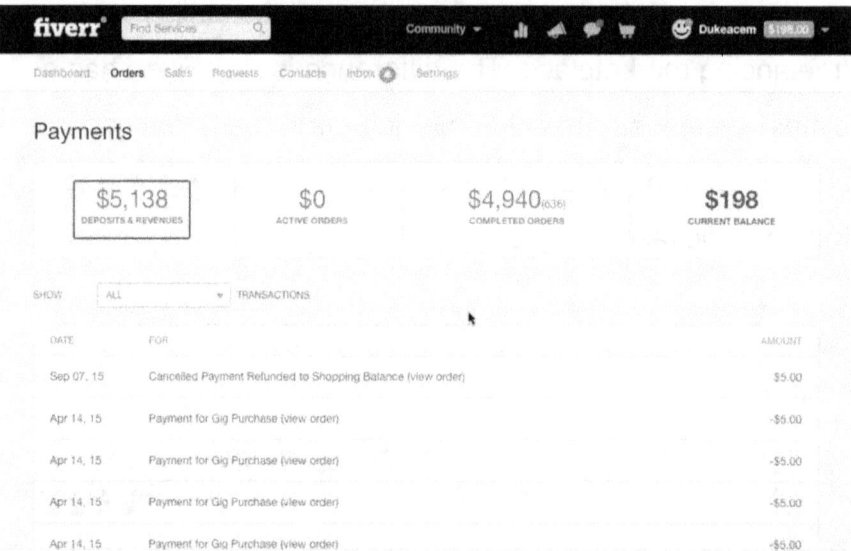

I've paid a lot of people all over the world to do little jobs for me.

Fiverr is great for things like when you need a *Facebook* cover or some simple job done like a simple video produced. There's all kinds of people on *Fiverr* that will do great work for you and it's really easy to make money on *Fiverr*.

I have not done much to make money on *Fiverr* and yet, I've made over *$300* with very little work. I only have five active gigs now and I don't do much with them. I don't make any attempt to promote them. Most of the sales I've made where earlier when I was on *Fiverr* more.

Fiverr is the very easiest place to make a little bit of money. That said, you are likely to need to do a lot of work in order to make more money of *Fiverr* just like anywhere else.

The nice thing is that *Fiverr* is a great tool that's easy to get started with and you can get to know yourself better. You can start figuring out what kind of gig you could make to earn *$5*. What will you be willing to do for 5 dollars?

That's the simplicity of *Fiverr* and that is why it works. People will spend money without being afraid. I've ordered a whole bunch of *Fiverr* gigs and it didn't work out, but it doesn't matter because it's only *$5*.

Between all of this combined, you can find at least one strategy, one place, where you can make a little bit of money to validate that you can earn money online.

Then, it might take another website for you to grow. You might be able to make your first or next *$5* on *Fiverr*, but then you might end up growing more using another approach.

Making social media and freelancing profiles that match your name

As you can imagine the more work you go creating new profiles online, the more chances you have that people find you if they hear about you or are talking about you.

If someone sees you on *Upwork*, you want them to be able to find you if you have a *Fiverr* profile, a *Facebook* profile, a *YouTube* channel or *LinkedIn*. You want people to be able to find you and the easiest way to do that is to get it setup all under your name.

I show you what I've done.

My *YouTube* channel is setup as *Jerry Banfield*.

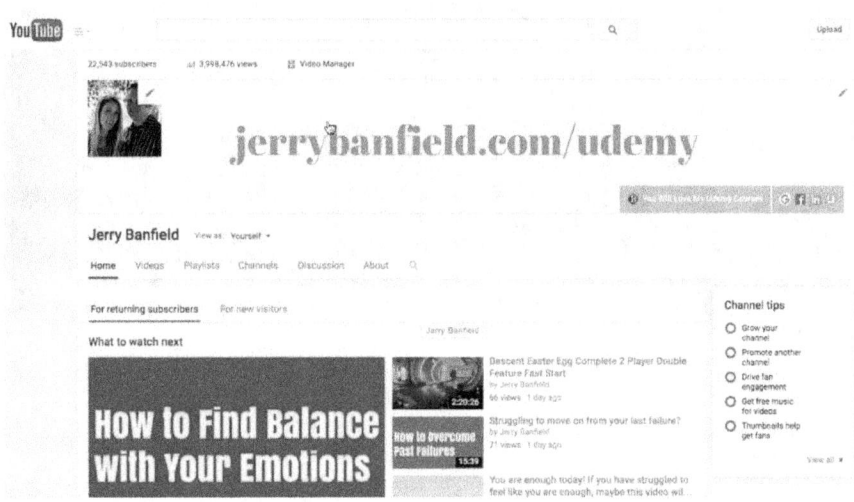

My *Facebook* profile is *Jerry Banfield.*

My company *Facebook* page is *Jerry Banfield.*

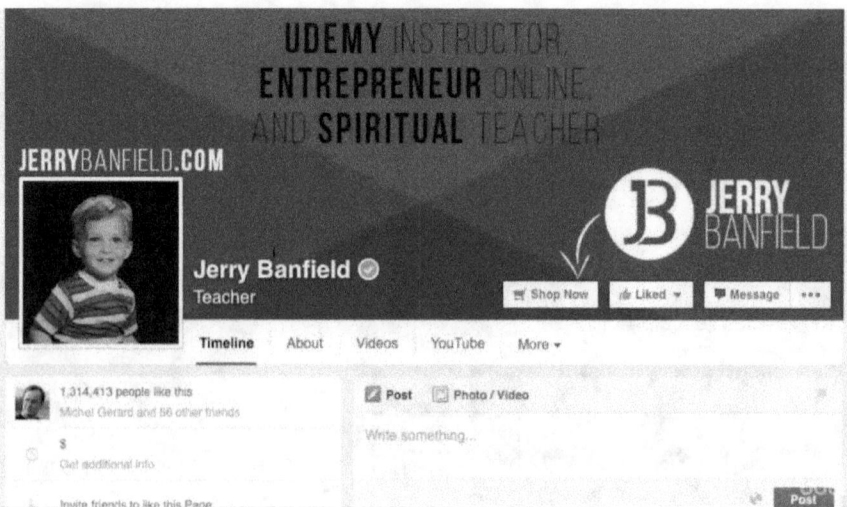

My *LinkedIn* profile is *Jerry Banfield.*

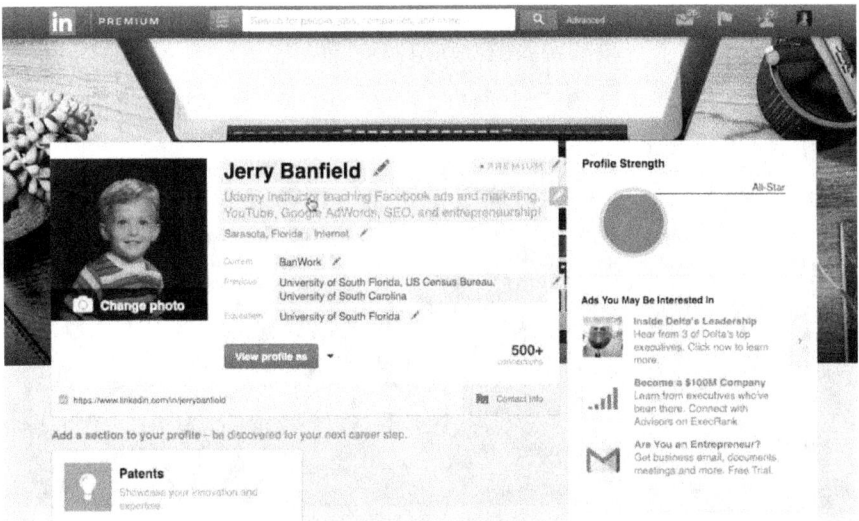

My *Twitter* profile is *Jerry Banfield.*

Even when I build new things now, I set them up with *Jerry Banfield*.

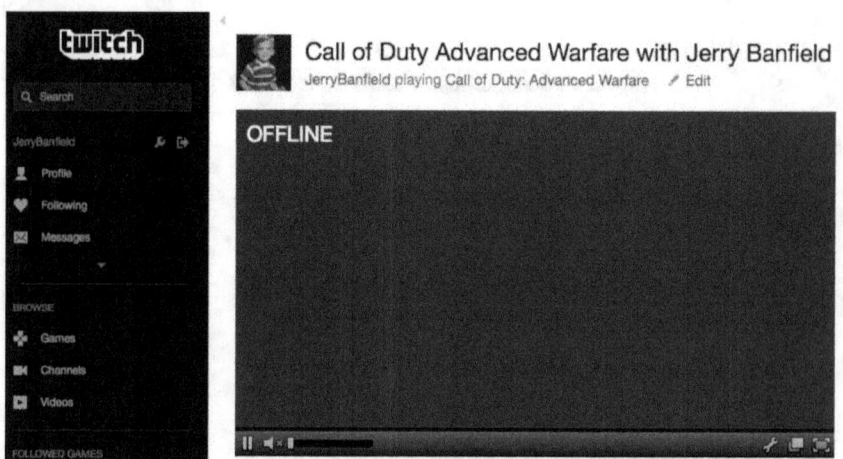

This was for video games before, but now I set it up for *Jerry Banfield.*

I want everything consistent so that if someone finds me in one place, they can go find me wherever they want to keep up with me.

Some people will find me on *YouTube* and then they'll end up following me on my personal *Facebook* profile or my business page. They may add me on *LinkedIn* or follow me on *Twitter*.

When you consistently set everything up under the same

name, then you get the most out of every person who finds you. People tend to want to get to know individual people.

I started off doing it with the company and it was a lot harder. Now, everything is branded under my name. Everything I do and all my profiles are under *Jerry Banfield*.

You'll still see some old ones if you search for me, but this is how I'm doing it now because this is what works the best.

I hope this is useful for you.

CHAPTER 2

Getting to know yourself is the most valuable thing you can do to make progress

In this second chapter of this book I am going to show you how you can get to know yourself so you can match what you can do and want to do with what other people need.

In the first section you will learn how you can *get to know yourself by answering some questions and finding your passion.*

The purpose of all these questions is to get you in a good mind state to make a strong foundation of your business:

Why are you working? What are you working for?

What have you done recently in your life for fun?

What would you do if you had enough money to do it?

What would you be willing to do for 20 years?

What do you hate doing?

What experience do you already have online?

Jerry Banfield & Michel Gerard

How does what you like to do match with why you do it and what people need?

This last question is certainly the most important in this chapter to position yourself as a freelancer. I invite you to meditate on these questions...

Get to know yourself by answering some questions and finding your passion

Knowing yourself is the biggest thing you can do to get a good start, or if you already got started, to continue better from where you are at. The more you know yourself, the less you have to work blindly in the dark, and the less frustrations and the less walls you have to hit.

One of the main problems I had getting started and growing for several years was that I had very little genuine self knowledge. I thought I knew and that was very dangerous because it turned out I knew very little about myself.

The more you know about yourself, the more you can match what you're doing and why you like to do it, with what people need. The key is what you're doing for other people. How are you out there helping someone else?

When you start thinking how you can help someone else, you will be amazed at how fast good things come back, and in order to do that you've got to know what you have to offer. You've got to know who you are and you've got to know what you've done.

There's so much to know about yourself in order to match

Jerry Banfield & Michel Gerard

up what you're doing with what people need to do that the easiest way, which also takes the most time and energy, is to get to know yourself. Once you know yourself, you can fairly easily start getting out there to who you need to be out there with.

This section and the following are about getting to know yourself with some simple questions. They seem simple at first, but the answers end up being deep when you go do them.

Each section in this chapter is just one question posed to ask yourself and think about. The purpose of all these questions is to get you in a good mind state to make a strong foundation of your business.

The most critical thing you can do is think right. You must have a good way of thinking to start with, and you can change that right now. You can work on, analyze and look at your thinking. Nothing is more important than how you are thinking about what you're doing online. If you're thinking about things in the right way, with service to other people, everything almost effortlessly will come together.

If you're thinking in a way that is self-centered and you try to go grab money like I was for the first several years of my business, if you're trying to go take things from people without regard to what they need, you'll continually be frustrated as I was.

I'm giving you the gift of right thinking that I've been given and that has allowed me to be with you. In the next two sections, I'll try and encourage you with some things to think about that can help you see where you at with your thinking and see some possibilities you might have never imagined for yourself.

Why are you working? What are you working for?

The first question is by far the biggest one.

Why are you working? What are you working for? Who are you ultimately working for?

This was very popular when I posted that question on the *Warrior* forum. This first part is about figuring out exactly the deepest reason why you are working.

I'm here writing this section out of the love and joy of being alive. That's why I'm here because I am grateful to be alive and I love being alive. I love life and that's why I'm here. I'm in a place now, this moment, that's beautiful, amazing and eternal.

I love life and for me a higher power is helpful for my understanding. I choose to call my higher power *God* out of convenience, and out of being raised with using that term.

You don't have to use *God* if you don't want to. It doesn't matter what you use because it's just a word. The word *God* is just a word the same as any other word. I find it useful to embrace that connection to a higher power and why I am working. Especially, in the sense that it helps me feel connected to all of humanity. It helps me feel the sameness that I have with all of humanity.

So the reason why I'm working is out of the love I have. Now, depending on where you are at, you might find your answer to why you are working.

You might find things like:

I want a new car, a new house and a better job.

I'm tired of my boss.

I want to provide for my family.

I want my kids to have an inheritance.

I'm sick of working.

I want to try something new.

Those reasons are all fine. I started out because I didn't want to be a professor anymore. I started out on a resentment because I lost a *$300* bet playing *Call of Duty* and I thought it was stupid how little money I had.

Then I thought that if I had a business online, I could probably make some real money, and then I wouldn't have to get all upset over losing a few hundreds.

That was a big part of why I started and everything I did corresponded to *"Why I was working?"*

The *Why* you are using with your work is the number one determining factor I can see of what outcome you'll get out of it. If you're working for a new car, you'll be lucky to get a new car and that will likely be a big part of what you get.

In other words, you're not likely to get a whole lot more than what you are working for. When you are working for all of humanity, you are working out of the joy of living. When you are working to be a good person right now and be of service, you'll likely can unlock your full potential for what you can really do.

This is so far beyond whatever I imagined. I'm in outer space right now compared to where I started, and yet, it's not that I am doing a lot different things.

It's because of the Why: I'm working because I love being alive, I'm grateful to be alive, and I'm here to serve you. I'm here to be useful to you. That's why I'm doing this and I'm doing it because it feels the right thing to do.

Your motivation to get a new house, make some new

money, have a new *X-BOX,* or to impress a future girlfriend or wife, husband, can get you looking deeper and deeper in them.

Why do I want a new girlfriend?

Why do I want to make money online?

I can get a hot girl, a hot car or a hot wife to feel good about myself.

Why do I want to feel good about myself?

I wanna feel like I belong to the human race.

Why do you want to feel like you belong to the human race?

I wanna be connected to everyone else.

Then you're right back to the higher power. You are already connected to everyone else. Thinking about why you're here trying to do what you're doing today will unlock your full potential, which is to be useful for other people and do things that other people need you to do.

I feel kinda like a drone lots of times today.

"Hi! What do you need me to do?"

I live now the best life I have ever remembered. I get up, I pray and I ask to be of service. I pray to take care of myself and be useful, and here I am. It's amazing!

When you think about the *Why*, you can unlock your full potential. I want you to unlock your full potential so you can be useful for me and do things that are good for all of humanity. If we all do our best with that, which ultimately we are doing, then we can have the best life together.

What have you done recently in your life for fun?

If you can match up what you do for fun with what you do for work, then you can have the best experience.

You'll enjoy learning the most and you can have a life today like I do where my work is fun. I love doing my videos and it doesn't feel like a chore or a job, or like I have to force myself to. I am just bursting with energy to do my videos. It's the same energy I had to play video games when I lived at my parents' house.

It might not always be obvious to ask yourself what is it you have done for fun recently or you like doing for fun. You often can somehow relate that to what you like to do for work.

In my case, I played video games most of my life for fun and my dad used to say that if I just could find a way to get paid for them, then I'd be in good shape. That's essentially what I've done. I've taken some of the things I like about playing video games, and then I found how to do them in my work.

I like the chance to work and to be online. I like being online and I like interacting in all these worlds online. I like learning all kinds of systems online.

That's fun!

I like to be able to talk and be myself, participate and feel connected online, which was good in video games. I like all the learning that comes with video games, all the different strategies and play styles. Now I'm even getting it set up so that I can integrate playing video games into my work directly, with the live stream. I've already done it with my *YouTube* channel at *www.youtube.com/c/JerryBanfield*.

The things I've learned from making videos for my *YouTube* channel, and from playing *Call of Duty* and other video games, have helped me to do better with my videos on Internet marketing topics and even my daily inspirational videos.

If you look at what you're doing for fun already, you might be able to find how you can integrate parts of it into what you are doing for work. You can combine that into something where your work and fun at some point blend together so much that it's hard to distinguish them.

What would you do if you had enough money to do it?

What would you do if money was not a consideration at all? What is it you would do if you didn't need to think it all about the money you'd make out of it?

I find that this question is really important for freelancing online and for doing your work because when you take the money out of it, only the thing itself is left to do.

I did a lot of things early on in my business that were purely money motivated. I didn't have a big desire to do *Facebook* ads for other people and I just wanted the money. Now, for the first time in my life, I am truly doing things that are not money motivated.

When you find the joy in what you like to do, you will find the ways to get the money to do it. If you try and do things for money, you'll often find you're doing things you don't like in order to get money. So imagine that you already have all the money you need to.

You can also do this as a scenario in the future and say, *"I already have all the money I need and I already made it!"*

"What am I doing? What am I doing in that scenario?"

Today, I am grateful that I am doing exactly what I want to as if money is not an issue. I love making my videos and I am even integrating ways to play video games that I enjoy. When you do what you do because you enjoy it, it's actually way easier to make money.

Now, it might take a little bit of time to get set up and it might take a lot of borrowed money to get in the position to make money. If you like doing it, you'll do those things though.

Imagine you just won the lottery, what would you actually do with it?

In this question, you might need to move beyond fantasy and look at a day. Otherwise, you might start off: *"Oh, I just won the lottery, I'd go to Vegas, I'd go to Hawaii, I'd buy a mansion or a building."*

Once you get passed those fantasies, you are in your mansion in *Malibu,* now what are you doing?

"Why? I'll sit around all day and smoke pot or something."

Well, if that's the foundation of what you do, you can find it through this question and you can look deeper.

How long would you do that for?

"Well, I might get tired of that after a year or two and I might start playing video games. Or I might start just talking to people."

The farther you can dive into what you would actually do if money wasn't an issue, the better. Then, you can start syncing that with what you are actually doing.

"If I had a billion dollars in the bank, I would be doing this. This is what I would do. I would keep making these courses. I would keep doing all the things I'm doing if I had a billion dollars and if I had no money at all, I would hope I could keep doing all the things I'm doing now also."

When you delete money from what you are trying to do, then you can start isolating what it is you really want to do. Money is a huge and powerful motivator that often poisons what you can see that you like to do.

I've done a lot of things in life. I thought I wanted to do them, but I was just trying to get some money. Jobs, careers, education, it has taken me a lot of self knowledge to put myself in a position where I'm doing what I do as if I had a billion dollars.

This is what I would do:

Make some videos, spend time with my wife and family and play some video games. Have some friends. That's what I'd do.

It doesn't matter where you do it, if you isolate what you would do, then you can better match what you do if money didn't matter with what you are doing when money does matter.

What would you be willing to do for 20 years?

This can help you to isolate schemes and hustling from your true purpose.

I would be willing and grateful to do what I'm doing now for the next 20 years. I would be honored to do the same thing that I'm doing today and it will be in slightly different forms. My daughter is likely to be older, I'm likely to be older and you are likely to be older. I'm willing to make these videos for my online courses and run my life as it is today for the next 20 years.

This is the first time in my life that I've ever been in that position and it's taken a lot of mistakes like doing a lot of things I did not want to do for 20 years. I was in law enforcement and I did not want to do that for 20 years. I went to graduate school looking at academia and I did not want to do that for 20 years.

Do I wanna do this forever? That's when I exited.

I had a 9-5 internship after college and I knew that I can't stand having an office job 9-5. I've never had one since then.

My wife somehow has had one for four years and it's hard.

Jerry Banfield & Michel Gerard

I wouldn't want to do that for 20 years.

I'm very happy doing what I'm doing now.

So if you ask yourself this question, it could help you make space in your life. If you already have a job that you're working at and try to add this on, or maybe transitioning, then you might need to get rid of your existing commitments first to make room for it.

If you have a full time job or a part time job that takes a lot of energy that you are not willing to do for 20 years, you might need the space in your life to really do what you want to do a hundred percent.

I know a guy who is trying to learn these things while he has a job because he can sit there all day in his office. He's a car salesman and he can be on the computer all day until a customer walks in.

If you find the space in your life and you honestly ask yourself:

Do I wanna sell cars for 20 more years?

or

Do I wanna try and be hustling online and slinging out all this random social media messages for 20 years?

No, I don't!

And I did that!

Do I want to be serving clients for 20 years?

No, I don't.

And that's why I don't serve clients on my business anymore. If you don't wanna do it for years, why would you want to do it at all. If the only answer is money, I guarantee that you can find something you will do for 20 years. Something that you'd like to do for years and that you'd love to do for 20 years.

You will find a way to make money at it if you make space to do it. It might not be easy at first, I borrowed *50* thousand plus dollars myself so that I could do what I wanted to do, what I liked to do and what I was willing to do for 20 years.

I borrowed the money for it so that I'll have time and space to just do it. Now it pays for itself, and I'm paying back the loans faster than I ever imagined. If you can look at and eliminate things that you wouldn't be willing to do in 20 years, you can open up a lot of space in your life.

You can fill that space with things that you would like to do indefinitely. When you're doing things that you would like to do indefinitely, it's absolutely amazing how easy it is to have great joy in the work you're doing.

I'm thankful for that I'm practicing that right here with you and I'd be honored to do this indefinitely. For ten years, you'd still be taking courses with me, read my books, watch my *YouTube* videos so we can continue growing together.

I hope I've given you inspiration to start looking around and figuring out what pieces of your life that you don't want to do forever you could delete, and which ones you would like to do more of.

I hope I've given you courage to start doing more of the things you are good at and that you like to do.

What do you hate doing?

If you find things you can't stand doing and you don't like to do, then you probably don't want to do them anymore.

If you have a hard time finding things you like to do, that can be helpful to at least find things you have to do so that you know not what to do. I know that finding what I hate doing when I mostly live in a positive lifestyle and mindset is kind of hard.

I know I hate going back and forth via email, I hate dealing with trying to schedule things and I hate feeling pressured or feeling that I have to do something new to be validated.

I also honestly tend to hate doing things that are brand new. I like to do things that are more comfortable and that I've already done before. I also, hate trying to make new relationships with clients who have lots of expectations. It's very stressful and it takes time to get to know each other.

I set things up now so that I don't get new clients. I make products so I can serve customers. I guess the difference is that the customer has just bought something, while with a client there is an on going service expected.

I love customers, but I'm not big on having clients. I learned that the hard way.

The more you ask yourself what is it you hate, the more you can dig deep into knowing what you shouldn't do, and then combine that with whatever you do know you like to do. This way you can get things and laser focused area where you can get started today, and figure out what other things you might like to do later.

What experience do you already have online?

Even if you have never worked online, you certainly have some experience which is not related to work.

When I started out in *2011*, you might have looked at me and think that I didn't have any experience working online. You might have said that I didn't know anything about business and about creating products. You might have told me that I didn't know anything about anything that matters for what I was trying to do because I had no previous experience.

I got that a lot like this and my own brother said that. I had lots of the same kind of comments come in and yet I already had a ton of really valuable experience, which took me a while to realize I had.

It's not a coincidence if I have one of the top *Facebook* courses online in the world because I also had one of the first *Facebook* profiles in the world back in *2005* when I was in college. I've used *Facebook* consistently for 10 years now and that experience matters.

I viscerally understand *Facebook* ads from the point of view of the person who's looking at them and that allows me to make ads that are very effective. That allows me to push the limits and do all kinds of things on *Facebook*.

When I started matching what I was doing in my business with my experience in *Facebook*, I was just doing what I already knew how to do: sending messages, making connections, adding friends and using the features on *Facebook*.

I realized then that I really knew a lot about *Facebook*.

Then, I was able to apply that experience in a way that drew clients at first. I made some money and now I create products out of it. I was able to use all that experience from *Facebook* to do things that people needed help with.

If you know all of your areas of experience, they all count, it doesn't have to be just what you do for work. I'm amazed how many people I see who think *work mode* and think completely separate *personal life mode.*

I played tens of thousands of hours of video games online since *2000* and even before that I was googling and dog-piling back in the day, and learning how to use these tools online.

I've been using the Internet a lot since the late 90s. That experience is extremely relevant and yet I never thought of it that way.

I didn't see the connection between playing lots of online video games and how that could be useful for my skills online. The better you get to know all of the things you do, not just your work things, but all the things you do, the more likely you can see areas of potential.

My experience with video games has given me a lot of visceral experience and knowledge with online systems and programs. When I go to do some new online system like *WordPress*, *YouTube* or some freelancing system, there are a lot of things that I unconsciously understand.

I understand things like how the backend works and I don't even consciously process it. The speed of which I can learn new things like *YouTube* is much faster because I am used to working with online systems. *YouTube* is just another online system and I can almost imagine how things were programmed on the backend.

I understand then what to test from there because I spent so many hours using so many online programs and systems designed by computer engineers, and using video games where there is a lot I can do unconsciously.

That allows me to learn rapidly in areas that are related to what you might call work. I understand where to learn, how to expand and what to test with a system like *Udemy* for example.

I have this visceral understanding of how things might be programmed that's not even conscious which just comes with experience.

That's why some people say: *"They're so good with their hands, they can fix anything."* My dad was like that and it's because he spent thousands of hours working with his hands, fixing things in all different scenarios.

You could throw him in on a random new scenario and he'd figure it out pretty fast because he had so much experience doing something else.

If you can count all of the experience you have across everything that you've done in your life, you'll find that you have a lot more skills than you ever imagined.

You'll find that everything you've done and all the learning in all areas of your life are relevant to whatever you want to do now, and whatever you might be able to do in the future.

Take a more broad inventory of yourself, really look and ask: *"What do I have experience with, especially working online, in both my personal life and work life?"*

How does what you like to do match with why you do it and what people need?

The purpose of this self knowledge is to get to know yourself so well that you can start thinking about what other people need.

You can start figuring out where you plug into that. There's an analogy of round peg, square whole or all those things. Think about it, you've got a very specific set up. You're not round or square, you're infinitely more complicated than that.

The question is where can you go find the exact right place to be a part of? There are all kinds of places in the world where your exact skills, your exact knowledge, your exact motivation and enthusiasm can be extremely useful.

Most people around the world have more talent than they would ever imagine. The question for you and for me everyday is how to match up how you can be of service to other people with why you're working and what exactly it is that you like to do, and will be willing to keep doing.

All of this self knowledge is guiding you into the next chapter where you figure out how you can most effectively take what you know about yourself and position it in a place where you can be of service to one other person at first, and then potentially more people.

If you don't know yourself, you can see how impossible this is. I've blundered through the first year of my business not knowing myself well enough to figure out where I should be positioned.

In a world where there is infinite positions, the best tool you can have is to know a little bit about where you should try and position yourself. The more self knowledge you have, the more effectively you can position yourself correctly.

CHAPTER 3

With your self knowledge, you can start learning what other people need

This first section of this chapter is all about thinking _what can you do for someone else that would really help them?_

When people have a problem to solve they get to work to find a solution to their problem. You might be the person that will provide that solution. Consider this question: _What problems are other people having now that you could solve?_

In order to solve problems other people are having it's important to have an in demand skill which has low competition.

What can you learn that is an in demand skill?

After you have identified your in demand skill and learned it, _where can you most effectively contact the exact right person you could help?_

Finally, the way you want to get paid is not necessarily the way clients want to pay you. In this last section I answer the question:

<u>*How are people used to paying for products or services*</u>
<u>*related to your offering?*</u>

Read on…

What can you do for someone else that would really help them?

This section is all about thinking what you could do for someone else that would really help them.

It's a drastic change of mind from *what can I do to make money* or *what can I do to get something for me?*

When you think like that you always try to take from other people.

With the self knowledge you have acquired from the last chapter, then you can put yourself in a good position because you know now more about yourself, what you like to do and why you like to do it.

You have to figure out who it is you could be really useful for. Ask yourself: *"Who could I help?"* In other words and at least this is my vision and goal, who can you be at the other end of this with helping?

In writing this I am trying my best to really help you and be of service to you specifically. You are who I hope I can really help and really be useful for. I hope I can give you the tools and give you the knowledge that I didn't have when starting out, so that you can do better.

This world is evolving fast and what you do online is getting competitive and is advancing so fast that you don't have time to mess around like I did. You can use exactly what I've already learned and come right along with me without having to blunder around for four years learning all these things the hard way.

You can see that I am doing exactly what I am asking you to think about now. I'm writing this thinking that I can be really useful and be of service to you.

What can you do to be in my position essentially?

I'm here to serve you. I am here to help you like a waiter in a restaurant. I am here to bring you what you need because it's about you. This doesn't accomplish anything if it's about me. You don't need me to talk about me for the good of me talking about me. You need me to do something for you.

If you are not into a place where you're thinking about what other people need, move your thinking and ask yourself, *"What does this person really need me to do for them?"*

What problems are other people having now that you could solve?

Some people are having problems right now that you specifically could solve. What problems are out there that you can help with?

I noticed that most of the time I was open to working with someone new, often I was open to visiting a new website, watching a new *YouTube* video, it was always a problem and it still is.

I've been trying to setup live streaming recently and I googled looking for answers, I watched *YouTube* videos and I read people's blogs. When I shop, I look at products and I read reviews. When I'm trying to do something new, I always go to work on the Internet.

That is where other people have the opportunity to get in front of me and make money from me.

Today, I just bought a new monitor. I saw it first time on *Best Buy* and I thought that I've never heard of that monitor before so I googled it.

One guy reviewed it really well on his blog and it's probably the fifth or sixth time I came to his blog. He did a very deep detailed review of two to three thousand plus words about that monitor. Everything you wanted to know about that monitor was written in the post. I clicked on his *"Buy Now"* button and then bought it on *Amazon*.

I'm not sure how much he made, but I would guess *10* or *20* dollars right there just sitting off his blog effortlessly. All he had to do is make the post and it's there indefinitely.

What can you do to be useful when people are struggling with problems?

One of the biggest traffic sources I have on my website is a post to help people with disabled *Facebook Ads* accounts. When people get their *Facebook Ad* account disabled, often what they'll do is google to look for help and for resources.

Then you know what happens? People find my post and they read it! Then they start looking and learning more about me: *"How does this guy know about this?"* Then sometimes, they end up buying my course.

Originally, most of the people who are enrolled in my *Udemy* courses have found me by searching for help for something on *YouTube*. I've done a ton of videos on *YouTube* about *Facebook* ads because that's for people who are looking for something new.

If you're not having a problem, if you're not in pain, most of the time you aren't going to go try something new and most of the time you're going to stick with what you know.

In my case, I mostly read books that are recommended by my friends. I'm not open to being solicited to read someone's book that I haven't heard of before. I'm not in pain about it and I can take it or leave it. When I'm in pain, I'm open to buying a new product right away to fix it.

When something's going wrong, I'm open right away. I've bought product after product to get my live streaming setup. I've read reviews and I've gone all over. So when you start looking around, you can just start with your problems.

What problems am I having?

What problems have I recently solved for myself?

One of the first big problems I solved for myself is how to get more *Facebook* likes cheap and that is the first thing I made a lot of money on. I realized, *"Oh, I've just solved a problem for myself that everyone else is having. I'd better help them."*

The problem was so prevalent that I was able to convert a $600 plus order straight through a *Facebook* message with a *Paypal* link.

When you look at the problems you're having, especially the problems you've solved, think that other people are having those problems too! The more you can get to know your problems and their solutions, the more you can understand exactly what problems other people are having.

You can then communicate a solution to them for those problems and in doing so they will come to you effortlessly. So what problems are you having today? What problems have you solved that you can help someone solve for themselves?

What can you learn that is an in demand skill?

Often, if you're talking to people and interacting with them in daily life, you will get these little tips and conversations that will help you answer this question.

You might not be able to answer it sitting still, standing or in the gym on a treadmill, but you might be able to answer it just by listening.

I did not listen very well for most of my life, and yet I heard a local business owner just give me exactly what I needed to know. I was talking to him about his business and he was telling me how he had paid some guy like thousands of dollars for some *SEO* work that was pretty much a scam.

Then, he ended up talking about how frustrated he was with his own *Facebook* likes and how other business owners had the same issue. What I heard was: *if you learn Facebook and how to build up a page, there's a huge need for help with that and there's extremely low supply.*

So what did I do? I went to work and I first learned. I found that I could buy fake *Facebook* likes on *Fiverr* for cheap. I put them on my page successfully before *Facebook* and *Fiverr* started cracking down on this.

So for a few months, I built a massive page because I tested it out myself. I learned to do it for myself and then I offered to do it for other people. That is how I started my business using *Fiverr* to buy *Facebook* likes for pages.

After just hearing a business owner talk about it, I was able to mark the prices up five, ten to twenty times. I'd buy for five dollars and I'd sell for *$50* to *$100*. Then, I realized that what people really needed wasn't fake *Facebook* likes because that was not what I needed.

What I needed was real *Facebook* likes, ideally for what you could pay for.

Then, where do you get that? You get that straight from *Facebook* ads.

When I realized through trying to do it myself that tons of people needed help with *Facebook* advertising, I understood that this was an in demand skill. If you know how to do this, a lot of people will be willing to pay you, and hundreds of people paid me to help them with this.

If you can locate this in demand skill that tons of people need help with, and that you can help with, then you'll be amazed at how easy it is compared to trying to struggle out there in the real world.

There is a lot of competition if you are trying to be an insurance sales man or trying to help with the same kinds of things everyone helps with, but when you isolate that in demand skill, there is almost no competition.

When I started learning *Facebook* ads, I was able to pickup clients so much faster than I've ever done before. It was absolutely unbelievable. So many people I have approached just said, *"Yes, thank you! I didn't even know I could even look for someone to help for this."*

So listening will help you with this a lot. Listen to what people around you are saying they need help with and at some point when you have enough self knowledge, you'll see a little idea bubble popping up and you'll realize that you could learn that in demand skill.

The lower the learning threshold is to get started, the sooner you can start picking up clients who will essentially pay you to learn. That's what I did with *Facebook* ads because I didn't get good doing it for myself, I got good by trying to do it for a bunch of clients. Then I got great at doing it for myself.

Clients all over the world essentially paid me to learn an in demand skill.

I know there's a course up right now showing how you can get paid to learn web development. You get paid by people to build websites and for every website you build, you learn how to build a better website.

The more in demand skill you can get, the better chance you have to actually get paid to learn it from the very beginning.

Where can you most effectively contact the exact right person you could help?

When you've got an in demand skill to learn or an idea, the next question to ask is *where can you contact or get in a relationship with people that need help with that?*

Usually it will be within the same medium and for me it was on *Facebook*. I have found that all I had to do was watch and look through all the ads I could see, then find the ads that were really crappy and low quality. Then, I clicked and messaged the page right when the page message feature came out, and said: *"Hey, I saw your Facebook ad."*

I would be nice about it and ask: *"How would you feel if I could lower some of your cost on Facebook ads based on my own success doing it for myself?"*

This sales pitch worked incredible with a fantastic cold conversion rate, straight through a message. People would often buy an advertising campaign without ever talking to me for as much as three-four hundred dollars, just off of that one little message.

When you get to know where people need help and what they need help with, then you can usually find a contact method. If you're trying to help people out with something, you should already know a little bit about it.

You can usually just network, you can find *Facebook* groups, local networking groups, mastermind groups or *Twitter* profiles. You can find all kinds of places where people are already talking and then you can reach the exact right person.

I have done a lot of spamming strategies and you don't want to do those. They are a lot of effort and you irritate a lot of people. When you can laser in on the exact right person to get a hold of, then you can do everyone a favor and not send out a bunch of extra messages.

Most importantly, do yourself a favor not to get a lot of negative feedback by finding the right person. This can take a lot of work, but the more you learn an in demand skill, the easier it gets and you are simply interacting.

This all matches up with your self knowledge. When you enjoy what you're doing, you'll naturally participate in things related to what you are doing. I went to an Internet marketing mastermind group locally and I learned a lot there. I was guided into doing *Udemy* more because I could see how much the founder of the group respected having a *Udemy* course up.

I didn't think it was a big deal at the time, but I got some really valuable learning out of it. Even if you don't get any clients or customers, you can really increase your learning by finding ways to interact with, and build relationships with people who are doing the same kind of things you are doing.

You want to build relationships with allies who you might call competitors. You want to get to know the other people who are doing what you are doing. You want to learn from them, so that together you can be the very best, and I have learned a lot from the top instructors on *Udemy*.

Some of what I learned has allowed me to be where I am now. I was inspired by other top instructors and instead of looking at them as competitors, I looked at them as examples.

When you do that, you'll be amazed before you're halfway through with what you get, and what you are able to give.

How are people used to paying for products or services related to your offering?

The habits people have related to whatever you are doing are really important because they dictate what people expect, and when you work on a way that people expect, then everything is smooth.

For example in *"do it yourself"* learning, people are in the habit of watching videos for free on *Youtube*, and then buying a course to get help, more hands on and to get higher quality content.

When people get services, they're often in the habit of paying for a fixed price service or paying hourly for ongoing work. When you try to do different arrangements, it gets to be challenging. I found that a fixed price service was a lot easier because people were in the habit of paying for a specific service, and for what I was doing, very few people wanted to pay hourly. They wanted to know they'd get a *Facebook* ad campaign out exactly as they wanted.

Now, I found that freelancers like to get paid by the hour. It's the opposite of what clients would want. So when clients are hiring, they like to know exactly what they are going to get in terms of service.

When people go to work they like to know exactly what they are going to get in terms of dollars per hour, so matching that up is often tricky.

When you know exactly how it works and whatever you are trying to do, then you can match what you are doing and how people are used to pay for it.

When I tried to get people to pay me hourly, it almost never worked because people wanted to pay for a fixed result like a finished campaign or ongoing management for campaigns. Almost no one wanted to pay me hourly, so I went with a service based approach.

All my efforts to get paid hourly were very frustrating and it was like no one was interested in giving me what I wanted.

When you set things up you want to set it up in a way that gives people what they want. I had a mastermind group before and people are not very willing to pay an individual to take their course directly.

People are much more willing to pay a company like *Udemy* and the individual is paid through them. When people buy products and services, they are in a habit of buying through a trusted store. *Udemy* is a very trustworthy store and it's much harder to get people to buy directly from you.

It's the difference between trying to sell your product in your own store and having your product in *Walmart* or *Best Buy.*

When you got your product in a trusted store, getting people in the door is almost effortless. The store itself will work to bring people in the door to buy your product. When you are trying to make people to come in your own store, you don't have a brand recognition and it's a lot harder to make sales.

In some areas, people are used to buying physical products on *Amazon* which is a great place to sell your physical products. People are used to buying on *Amazon,* and trying to sell them directly through your own website can be a lot harder.

The way to get to know how people work is to watch how you work. I get a lot of questions and people saying, *"Jerry, your courses are so valuable, they have so much information, why don't you offer them for a thousand dollars or two thousand dollars on your own website?"*

My answer is that I don't buy that way. I don't buy anyone else's expensive course. I buy cheap courses and I buy cheap audiobooks.

That's how I do my learning. I don't like buying and I do not buy expensive courses or exclusive products. I buy stuff that's cheap and that's proven to work for other people.

So that's how I set my business up. I used to try things in a subscription basis. I tried to get clients to subscribe every month or to pay me a recurring fee to do their ads every month, and that didn't work because most people wanted to just pay on a one time basis.

It was a lot harder to get subscriptions than one time orders. For the biggest business I've got, I started with a small order and worked my way up. People very often will start with a small order and work their way up. Most people don't want to start with a new person doing a huge order.

If you get to know how you operate, you can set up what you do for other people in a way that matches what you do. If you buy two thousand dollar courses from people, you might be able to make one and sell it. If you don't buy *$2,000* courses from other people it's probably not going to work for you to try and sell one.

If you have to get everything for free and don't buy other people's courses, it might be hard for you to sell your courses. I didn't do a good job selling my courses when I used to learn for free. When I started buying other people's courses, guess what? I started selling more.

If you wouldn't pay anyone else to help you out with a part of your business and perform a service for you, then why would you expect someone else to hire you to perform a service for them?

If you are trying to help out in *Facebook* ads but you are trying to do graphic design yourself even though you are terrible at it and obviously need help, then why would people hire you to help them when it's clear you can't hire anyone to help yourself?

When you do what you want to get, then you'll get what you want. So if you give what you want, for instance if you go hire other freelancers to do graphic design, to help with your website and to help you get various things set up, then it's reasonable to expect that other people will hire you to do the same thing.

If you are not willing to do whatever it is you're trying to do for other people, it's unlikely you'll succeed. When you set your business up in a way that's consistent, when you learn how people are used to working in this situation you're trying to be in, whether it's customers or clients, you have a much better chance at getting yourself setup correctly in the details and execution of whatever you are trying to do.

I hope that asking you how people are used to buying products and services, and what you're doing and how you are used to doing it as a customer, is helpful for you.

CHAPTER 4

Build a foundation that attracts new clients and customers when you start

Starting a business online is challenging and the best state of mind is to _assume you will get no clients and customers to start and be grateful for leads_.

I will show you in this chapter how I did to _attract new clients effortlessly instead of depending on promotion_ and how you can do the same.

When starting a business, frustration can come in different flavors, but _instead of being frustrated, appreciate your free time and use it to learn_.

Having no clients and customers when starting brings its own limitation, and I'll show you that _having clients and customers brings its own set of limitations_ too.

Before you get a ton of clients to serve on a daily basis, _use your free time to build a YouTube channel, WordPress website, and more!_

Read on...

Jerry Banfield & Michel Gerard

Assume you will get no clients and customers to start and be grateful for leads

Welcome to building your foundation for your entire freelancing business online. It could be the future for you the way it is the present for me. You might be able to work full time online with a strong foundation that you can start building today or you may have already worked on.

This section is guiding you gently into the work to build your foundation and the nice thing about it is that it doesn't require clients or any customers. It's a strong foundation mentally, and then build out on building a strong presence online.

Now when I started out all I could think was that I got to have customers and clients. You more than likely won't get any customers or any clients starting out. It took me months to get any clients at all, even one. I spent hundreds of hours of work agonizing, frustrating, thinking and wishing I could have some customers to validate me.

You don't have to make that mistake. You don't have to look at it that you need customers and clients to get started. You can do a lot of great work and if you just assume that you are not getting any customers or clients getting started, then you can be grateful for any leads you get.

You can look and structure your time around the potential to build a great profile and to build a great presence online that will effortlessly attract customers and clients instead of having to go out there and hustle for them.

That's what I have right now. When I started out, one of the things I did right was to put a lot of effort into making my website and to put a lot of effort into learning. That is why you are reading this book.

If you assume that it's going to be hard, the hardest thing to do is go from zero clients or customers to one. That is harder than any other step because you are just in the dark. So if you just assume that you are not going to go from zero to one for a while, then you can use that time to build a strong foundation that will allow you to go from zero to one, and from one to two, and from two to three and so on.

If you accept that getting started is challenging and you work with that, you can use whatever free time you have. Then you can build a strong foundation online.

Attract new clients effortlessly instead of depending on promotion

Here is a powerful thought that can help you a lot with everything you're doing. If you can think attraction rather than promotion, you can do amazing things in terms of getting clients and customers with very little effort.

You do not need the anxious struggling efforts that I spent trying to get customers, sending thousands of messages out on social media and running all kinds of ads.

Attraction means that when people need you, they will be attracted to you and they will come to you. Of course at this point you might be thinking how you are going to attract people if you don't have anything setup, but you want to think attraction from the very beginning.

Wherever you are at, whatever beginning you've made already, you want to think attraction.

I think attraction and almost every thing good that's happened is out of attraction. I'm very confident that you are reading this out of attraction. I didn't hit you with an ad, but you might have found me on some organic method on *Udemy*, or you found me on some *YouTube* search or suggested video. That's how almost all of my students come in and that is attraction.

Now if *Udemy* ran an ad, I count that as attraction because if I'm not paying for it then that's attraction as far as I'm concerned. So if you found this book from my blog, my *Facebook* page or through *YouTube*, more than likely you were attracted to me. So I'm preaching what I'm practicing.

I run ads also that mainly help with promoting the attraction. When I advertise a *YouTube* video the whole idea is to get it to rank organically higher. So what I'm saying is that attraction is so much more effective than promotion that it is hard to believe.

Promotion is when you are sending messages or paying for ads that are only good if people convert on them. They are not paid ads that just help organic ranking or something, but ads designed to make a sale.

When you are paying for ads like this on *Facebook,* if people don't convert it's wasted and it's gone because you don't get any lingering effect. You may be like I was, sending thousands of social media messages all over the place where I was promoting myself.

All I could think of for the first several years of my business was how to promote myself. If you can start with attraction, start with the idea that you want to sit where you are, and build things so that people come knock on your door, metaphorically speaking.

If you can think that way from the start you will have a gigantic strong foundation and you will look around and see work you can do that will build attraction instead of promotion. The problem with promotion is that when you are trying to first get going, even if you've been going a little bit, when you are trying to promote yourself what you are usually promoting is honestly not that good.

I tried to promote all kinds of amazingly awful low quality things over the last three years. Even if you can make a beautiful website and have everything look professional, you usually won't have any social proof to go along with it. You won't have any client case studies and you won't have any reviews on your existing product. You won't have a bunch of people who give word of mouth referrals.

Getting started and growing is difficult. If you think attraction to start with, you can put your effort into building attraction on purpose. Things like *YouTube* videos or *Udemy* courses which will draw people to you.

In the beginning you have so much time, energy and effort that's open. Focusing on attraction will allow you the best long term results. Now, of course, attraction takes long term work and a lot of people don't like to wait for good things to happen.

I went out promoting myself because I didn't want to do something that might work in a year, but the best results I've ever gathered are with doing things that might work in a year, planting a lot of good seeds all over the place watching which one grows and going back there.

For the first year or so on *Udemy,* I hardly made anything. Once the seeds grew, I got a thousand a month. When I hit that, I realized that if I did this all the time, it would make enough to pay all of my bills. It took more months before it started to even pay close to enough. I borrowed a bunch of money so I could just use this money to make up the difference.

Now it pays unbelievably well and it took close to two years to get it setup really well. If you can start with something like that in mind you might be able to save yourself two, three, four or five years. You might even avoid the failing of your business.

Starting with attraction is one of the most powerful mindsets you can go into this with. The idea that everyone must come to you and that you can't go just bang down doors, hustle, run and go get clients. You have to get people to come to you and I do that now.

Everything I do is setup for that. I use a promotion to assist attraction sometimes, but almost everything is done through attraction.

Instead of being frustrated, appreciate your free time and use it to learn

A big part of your foundation is how you feel about what you are doing. A common characteristic, based on my experience and from all the questions I have received online, is that getting started is really frustrating because there is no validation there.

You don't know what you are doing and you don't have any clients or customers. You are trying so hard to work and being something more than you are right now that it is frustrating because ultimately in the deep spiritual level, you can ever be any more than you are right now.

Now is all we really ever have and going along with this can help you get over the frustration that you have to be somewhere else to make what you're doing now worthwhile. In the beginning it is very common. I was so frustrated getting started. I was always plotting and scheming on how someday it'll be basically like this. I was always fantasizing and I was miserable doing what I was doing.

It didn't get to where it is now until I was happy doing what I'm doing. You can tell I'm happy doing what I'm doing, I love making courses and books to share with you. Nothing good started happening until I began working from a place where I was already happy.

As long as I put the frustration into my work, I never could get anywhere. I've got hundreds of clients and yet, I still was frustrated. I thought I should be in a better place and I end up losing all of those clients and all of the money I spent trying to grow from having those clients.

As long as you are frustrated you will be lucky to learn anything and you will mostly spin your wheels. Sometimes you will spin your wheels and they will take you places, and yet you will end up wrecking the places you go and the client relationships you have.

Frustration is hating the moment, feeling like it's not good enough and that you are not enough. It poisons all of the work you are doing and if you can see that, all you have to do is notice.

"Oh, ok, I'm really frustrated and I am sitting there today feeling like I'm not good enough."

I'm learning to do live streaming right now and it comes with a lot of challenges. I looked over and over last night for a new capture card because my *$200* capture card doesn't work with the *$1,000* software I have. It is challenging to learn and do something new, but the point is I enjoyed the learning out of it.

I used to get so frustrated that my wife thought it was a nightmare. I was going to try something new and I used to flip out, bang the table, scream, cuss and go crazy. I've pounded the keys off of a keyboard before and that's how frustrated I used to get. As long as I got frustrated with what I was doing, I wouldn't learn and learning new things is critical!

Learning is the core of what you are trying to do and frustration blocks learning. So here is a way that you can look at to get out of frustration: *You can find gratitude for the good things you have right now.*

That's what works for me along with a lot of prayers and going to a support group everyday. I put a lot of effort into not being frustrated by doing good things and being grateful in my life because when I'm frustrated, I keep making it worse.

The easiest thing that you can be grateful for now is the free time and opportunity you have. *Udemy* has been so demanding that it's been almost a year since I had time to learn something new about instead of just simply teaching what I already knew about. To be fair, I've been learning the whole time, but it's been a year since I've had time to really dive into learning something new and challenging like live streaming.

You have the ability to learn and do something right now. Even if you are working already and if you are trying to build what you're doing, you will likely have much more time now. If you don't have enough time when you're trying to do this and you really want to do it, you might need to make time.

I quit my job in order to do my business full time before it was making even enough to pay for itself. I quit my job because I knew I needed more time. Having more time to do things is something worth being grateful for.

You might say: *"Look, I've got to have clients, I got to have validation and I got to have customers."*

When you get all those things, you'll have less time and less choices about what to do right now. I have enough responsibility on *Udemy* that it is somewhat dictated to me as the first choice.

Now the way I live, I have the freedom to choose things that are right and that are good for me. At the same time, I have so much responsibility on *Udemy* that it is the first thing I have to do all the time now.

Enjoy the chance to learn so many things and to really explore, enjoy the chance to try some things like making *YouTube* videos. Ultimately, the most valuable thing you can do is learning. You are more than likely now to have more time and energy than ever to learn.

When you get customers or more clients, you won't have as much time and energy to learn. The reason I'm here with you is because I dumped a ton of time and energy into learning all kinds of different things. If you can do the same thing then you can get around being frustrated.

If you were learning how to do boxing you'd get punched in the face a lot of times and learning to do these things online is very much the same, but if you accept that, this means you are learning and that's good!

Then, you don't have to be frustrated like I was so much. It's a miracle that I was so frustrated and still managed to keep going. Frustration will often take you completely out of the game.

In *2005*, it took me out of the game for six years. I gave up and said: *"You know what, I don't have what it takes to make money online. I don't have what it takes to do anything except to have a regular job."*

For six years, I didn't even consider trying again because of the frustration I had. I'm here to tell you that frustration is normal and it's worth working on, looking at the good things in your life, working on finding gratitude for what you have right now just as it is.

A power thought that helps my friend is: *"You're right where you're supposed to be."*

This can help a lot with your frustration. You're right where you're supposed to be. If you were supposed to have a *100,000* customers or if you were supposed to have *100* clients, you'd have them now.

You've got right now what you need right now and when you are ready for *10,000* students on *Udemy*, you'll have them. When you are not ready for it, you won't have them. That makes things a lot easier for me. I'm not ready for *100,000* students on *Udemy* and I'm ready for exactly the number I have today, and I'm grateful for that.

I'm not ready to start live streaming, but I'm ready to learn about it and to get it setup today. I don't have to be frustrated that I am not live streaming today because I'm learning about it. I'm building a strong foundation upon which, I can make a great live streaming channel.

Having clients and customers brings its own set of limitations

One thing that might be helpful to know upfront while you are looking for more clients or customers is that you can look at it as a limitation when you're getting started. The nice thing to know is that having customers and clients brings its own set of limitations as well.

Having more than *60,000* students on *Udemy* brings lots of limitations. I don't even check my own email anymore. I have so many responsibilities with my existing customers that I have been greatly encouraged by all of the work I have to do to get help with it.

I have to give up then all the things I exclusively did. I have to share and open up my life, things like my *YouTube* account and bank account. I have to open up things for other people to do work and help me out so that I can have enough time to serve my customers effectively.

Having more customers and clients brings limitations to it and if you have a bunch of clients and customers, you'll see that it is just as limiting as having very few or no clients and customers.

My wife has a job she can go to *40* hours a week and while she is there, she works. When she is at home, she doesn't work. When you have clients and customers, you're liable to be working all the time. When I had a lot of clients, it was worst than having a job. My clients wanted things all the time, Saturday and Sunday sometimes, and they sent emails frequently.

Having clients is very limiting because it restrains you from being able to do things like making videos. It limits you from being able to run your own schedule lots of times. When you have several clients flip out on one day, it will take a lot of your real time and energy. Having customers can be the same way depending on exactly how you've set it up.

It takes a lot of love and maintenance every single day to work on my *Udemy* courses. In fact, it's challenging for even taking one day completely off *Udemy* like not making any videos, not answering any questions and not thinking about it or planning on how to do something different.

It's challenging for me to even take a day off, so what I do is not to work too much one day. That's the easiest way for me not to get burnt out.

What I hoped I communicated is that you will have

limitations no matter what you are trying to do. I had the idea before that my life will be limitless and wide open if I had tons of clients and customers. I very foolishly thought that and ran towards it, and then found the hard way that I have now a completely different set of limitations.

I liked my limitations better when I had fewer clients and customers. I hope you don't have to make the same mistake of trying to get so many clients and customers to validate yourself, and then to only discover the limitations are often more challenging to work with than what you already might have without clients and customers.

Use your free time to build a *YouTube* channel, *WordPress* website, and more!

Now that you know yourself better and that you understand a little bit more about what you can contribute, and see the limitations that will come in the future with executing well in the present, you should be in a state where you are ready to get to work presenting yourself online.

You can put the free time and energy you have into making great social media and freelancing websites profiles.

Learn more about yourself and anything you think you might want to help other people with. Your opportunity to learn is in the perfect place with all this free time and your opportunity to present yourself professionally to the world is now.

It's right here.

If it's not right here because you have existing commitments, you may need to cut some of those commitments to make room for it. If you really want to have the kind of lifestyle I do where I can live and work at home anytime on any schedule, I hope this chapter has motivated you to get in a place that took me years to get to the hard way.

You can start right now on your *YouTube* channel, *Wordpress* website, on your freelancing and social media profiles, you can use all this time to look really good online and to attract clients to you instead of having to go out and get them the hard way like I did.

CHAPTER 5

YouTube is the easiest way to attract people to you and grow consistently

Do you have your *YouTube* channel setup? In this chapter I will show you how *YouTube* can help you find work online.

Showing ads on *Facebook* is not always the best timing as people are not actively looking for what you may offer. *Timing is everything in life. Get found on YouTube at the right time* when people are searching a solution to a problem that you can solve.

If you haven't started your *YouTube* channel yet, *zero to one video uploaded is the biggest step on YouTube* and you can do it right now.

Talking head videos are the easiest to make and a great way to start and you can start speaking to the camera without script from your heart like I do.

Screen capture tutorials are the foundation of my success on YouTube and out of my ten top videos, nine are screen capture videos.

You can build yourself a great *YouTube* channel for your freelancing portfolio.

Read on...

Timing is everything in life. Get found on *YouTube* at the right time

Timing in life is everything and yet most of us work online out of good knowledge of what it is in terms of how it impacts you. Timing is what makes *Facebook* ads and most things on *Facebook* very hard to do.

Look at this ad below. It is likely costing anywhere from *2* to *10* cents for *HubSpot* to show it to me and it is at the wrong time.

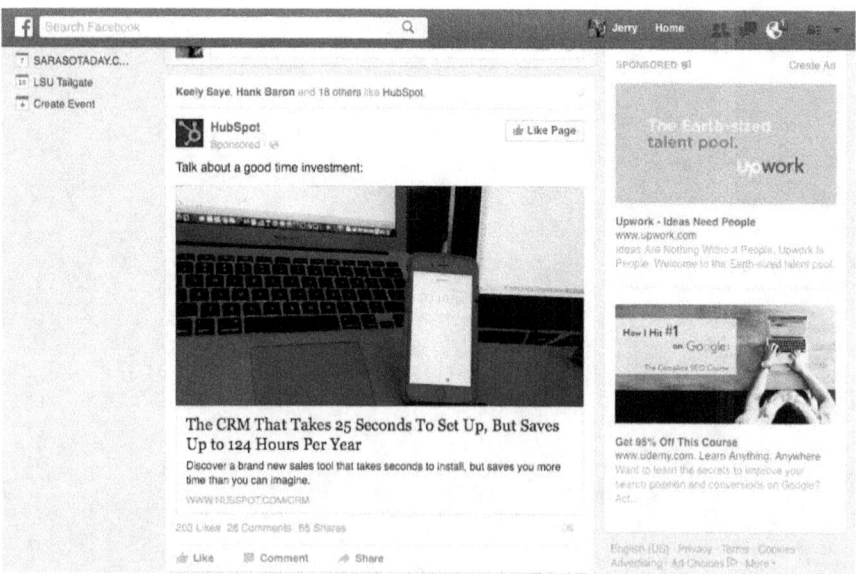

Although I guess that it's theoretically at the right time if you instantly go there. When I'm using *Facebook*, I see a lot of things that are useful when I'm not looking for them.

I see a bunch of things that are interesting that I just scroll by. I just keep scrolling until I see some interesting posts. You know, maybe someone's gotten married or various things, but most of the time I just kind of thoughtlessly scroll. I read little things and then you know what I do?

Bye! I'm gone!

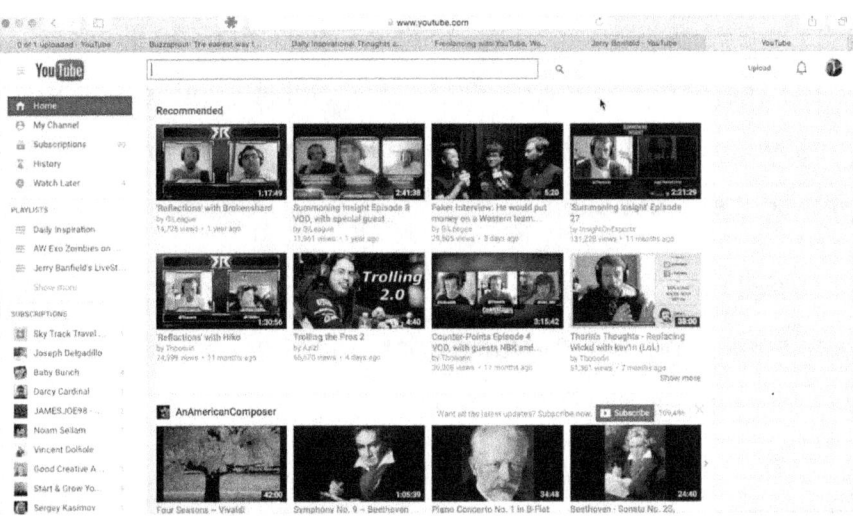

On *Facebook*, I'm not usually doing anything that's valuable for other people, I'm just kind of messing around as you can say.

On *YouTube*, when I'm looking for something, I am in the

mood. Think about dating. If you try to pick people up at the wrong place and at the wrong time, you can totally get back nothing at all. If you are at the right place and at the right time, it's absurdly easy to meet someone new and make a lasting connection.

Working online is the same way and here is an example. When I need help with something I can go to *Google* or *YouTube*.

On *Google*, what do I search for? Well, if I need flights somewhere, I search *Google* for predictable queries that are mostly the same that other people have already thought and shared the information.

What am I looking for in *YouTube*? I'm looking for real help with something. On *YouTube* what I might be looking for is a *microphone for YouTube videos*.

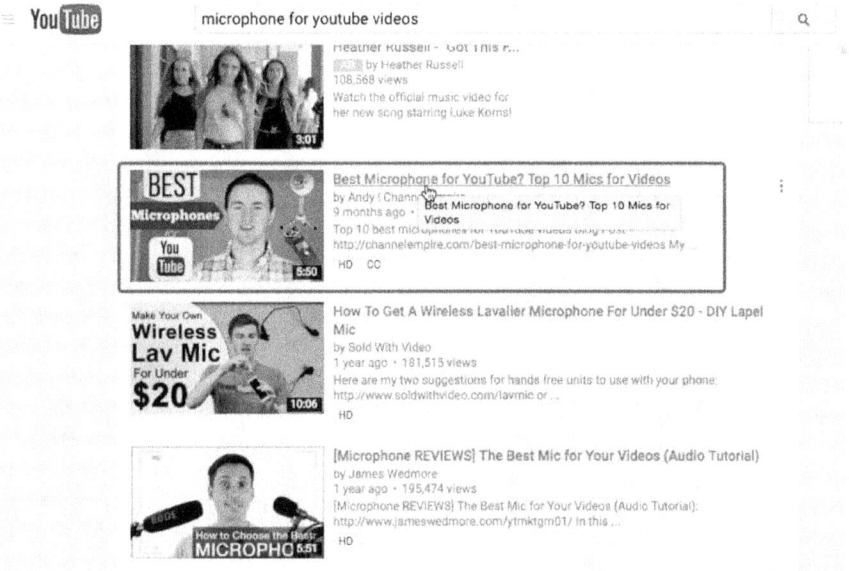

This isn't something I need, but this is the kind of search that I've done a lot of in the past. Right there I've got a video from someone I've never heard of before.

This mic right below is one that I use and you can see that I actually watched this video before.

I never heard of this guy the first time I searched and then I watched a lot of the videos he made.

The power of *YouTube* is to actually get people to find you when they need you. I'll give you an example. If you type in *Google AdWords tutorial* you can see that I've got a *Google AdWords tutorial* on this first page.

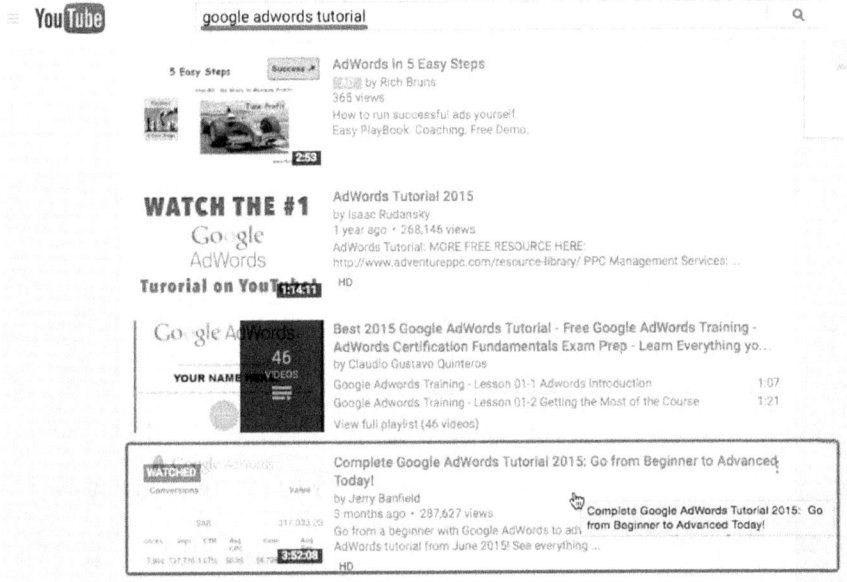

That's a three hour video that makes sales almost everyday.

Now if I type in something like, *Hacking for beginners 2015*, if you scroll pass the ad there is a video I have up with *773,000* views on it.

It's right there for the people who need it when they need it. Imagine me trying to go find *700,000* people to watch that video. Impossible right? There is no way I could possibly do that and yet, all I have to do is put it in *YouTube.* Of course, if you want to push up to the very top like this, then you may need to run ads on the video, but it's that simple.

You show what you can do on a video you put on *YouTube* and there is volcanic potential. That is not just going to happen through most of the other method you'll try and use online.

I believe that *YouTube* is the top tool for freelancers online. When you search for *"Jerry Banfield,"* you go straight to my channel at *www.youtube.com/c/JerryBanfield*.

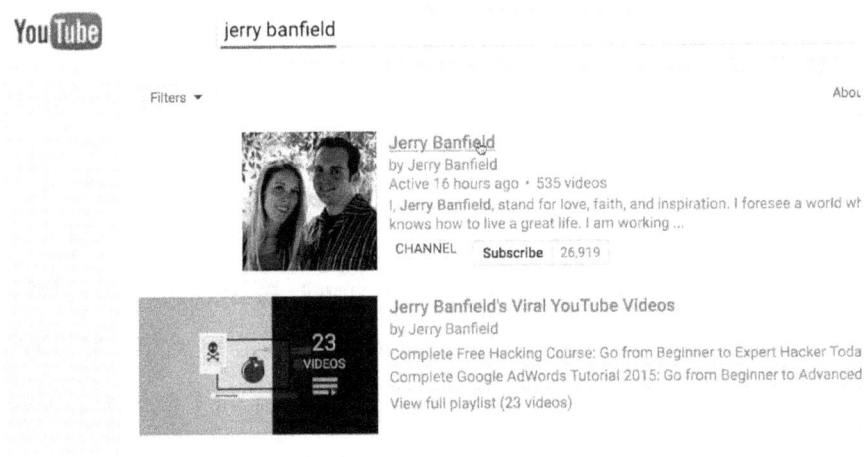

Then, on my channel I've got a list of viral *YouTube* videos I made with *100,000* of views.

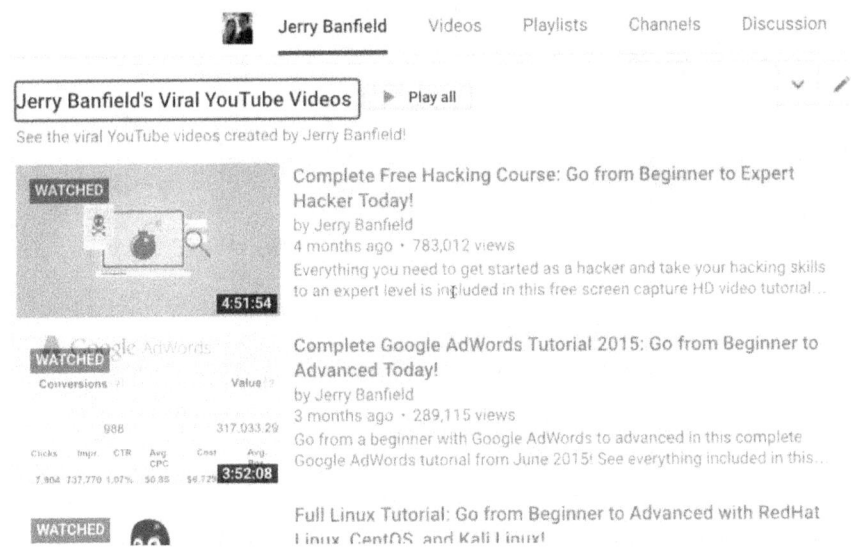

I can get people watch my other videos and then I get

sales. The sales make themselves and I don't even have to actually do anything because the sales come straight through my website.

This is what's possible as a freelancer online when you think about getting people to come to you at the right time. *YouTube* is the best place I found for that and I looked at a lot of different places. You can see I'm practicing it for myself with *26,000* subscribers and a half million plus views.

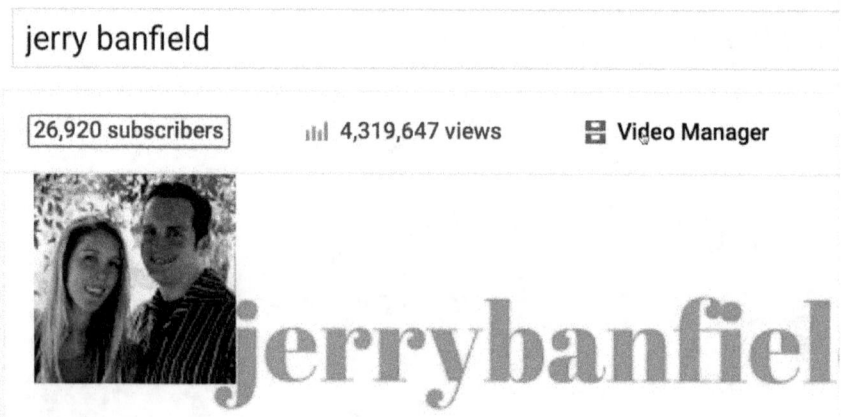

YouTube is amazing and it will give you opportunities so far beyond what you ever imagined if you are willing to try and make some videos, and put some effort into it.

Zero to one video uploaded is the biggest step on *YouTube*

The biggest step you can take on *YouTube* is get your very first video uploaded. It's just like that first step we took on the moon. One small step for man, one giant leap for mankind. It might be one small click for you to upload a video on your channel once you've got it created.

YouTube always changes the interface to create the channel so I trust you can create the channel with whatever interface *YouTube* has setup.

Then, you click that upload button and the screen comes up like this.

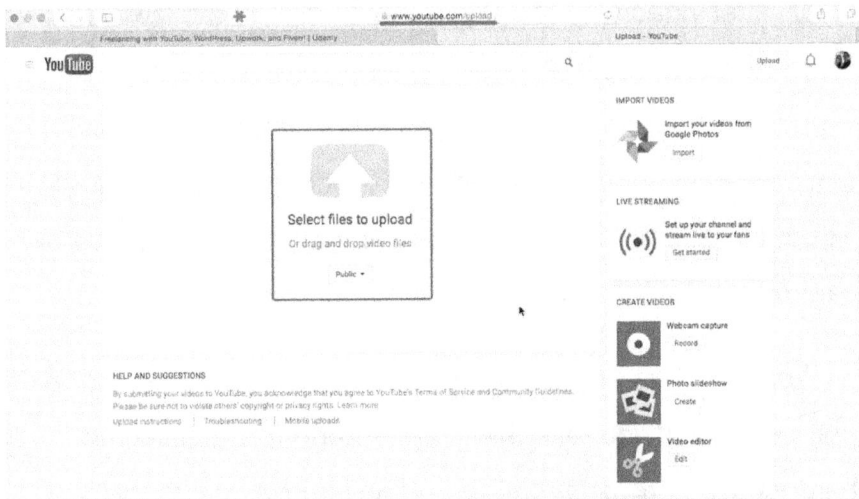

The biggest thing you can do if you want to be successful on *YouTube,* or just want to see if it's right for you, is uploading that very first video. You will be amazed at what's possible after you upload the first video.

Most people in the world do not have a *YouTube* channel. Most *YouTube* channels don't have any videos uploaded to them, or they have very few. So immediately if you upload one video, it's a giant step. Any step you take will be smaller than that in the future.

I encourage people in my *YouTube* course to just upload any video and I'm encouraging you now to upload any video just to break the ice and to get the learning started.

My first video was literally on how to say the *"F"* word different ways. Yes, that was my first video on *YouTube* and it is private now. That was literally the first video I uploaded. If I can be here with you today after uploading that as my first video, there is no reason you can't upload just any video you can make. Get it uploaded and then take another step.

YouTube has huge potential for you. You can only realize that potential if you take the first step and it is usually the hardest. It's hard, scary and you don't know what's going to happen. You don't know how people are going to react to your video. You don't know what your friends are going to think. You don't know what someone from Vietnam is going to say when they come and drop a comment on your video after they have watched it.

Doing something new is scary and the only way to get better at it is just to make some videos and get people's feedback. No one was very impressed with my first video and even my friends just laughed at it. They weren't impressed with my initial *20 to 30* videos and yet that's how I got to today.

Now, I've made thousands of videos and you are not alone taking that next step either. I just uploaded this video *26* minutes ago.

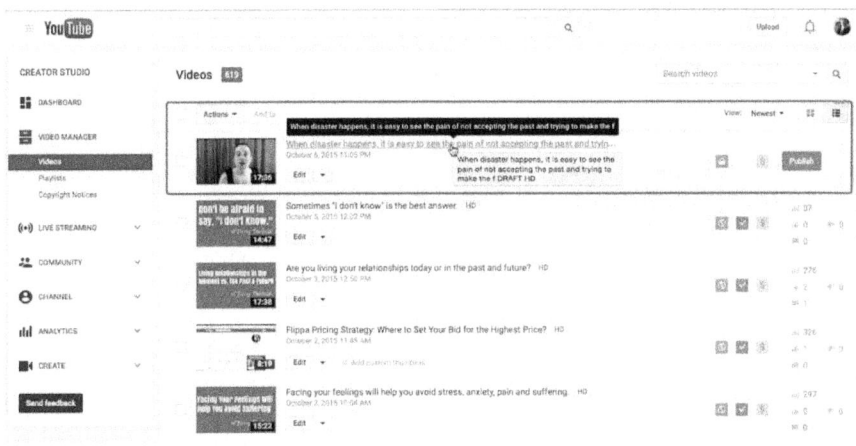

It's waiting for my team members to go in there and get it published.

I have the courage to do this almost each day. You can see that I upload *YouTube* videos on a regular basis below.

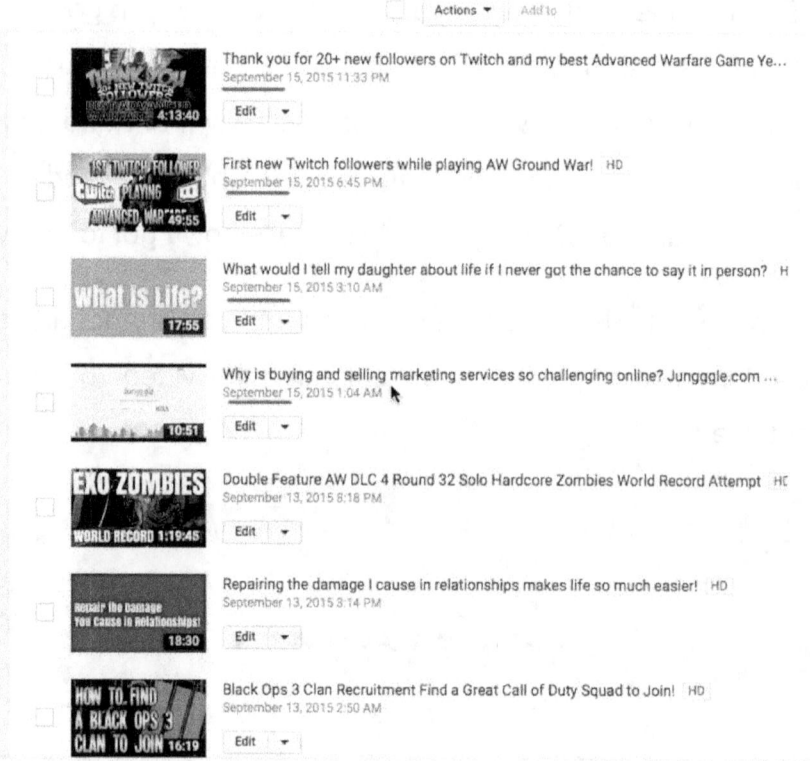

If I can do it I think you can do it too!

Talking head videos are the easiest to make and a great way to start

Talking head videos like this where you've got your head in the screen somewhere and you've got any kind of background, are one of the easiest things to get started with because you can make them with any smart phone, almost any laptop or computer you have.

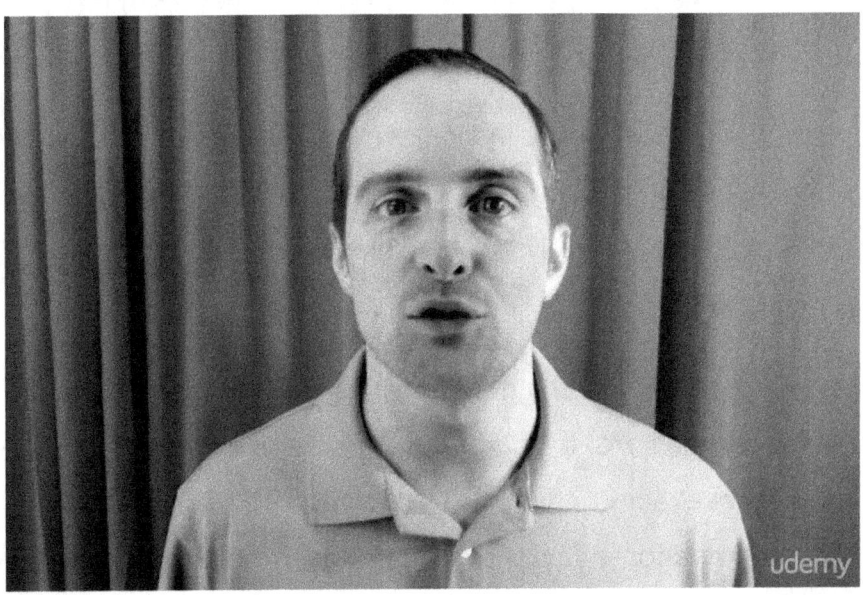

These videos are very personal, honest and straightforward. I like to do them with no script and just talking straight from the heart.

You can't compete in the world of scripted mind games

because there are more people that have more resources and more time to write out all these perfect scripts. What you can do is offer straight from the heart honesty in whatever video you are making about a subject that relates to exactly what you are doing.

The beauty is all you have to do is turn your camera on and start talking. If you say a lot of *Uhms* and *Ahhs* and you can't stand to watch yourself talk, put the video up anyway. You will get better I promise.

What I do now is a reflection of me having done thousands of these videos and believe me lots of people still have plenty of negative things to say like how my nostrils flare when I do various things.

I have a kind of a rhythm almost behind my talking speed that people criticize. It kind of reminds me of *Obama*, like you can almost exactly hit when he is going to say every word. I guess other people say I have a talking rhythm also that can be repetitive, and yet it's almost like a song in a way. It keeps you interested and takes you along with it.

Whatever it is, it's developed over time with doing a lot of these different videos, or getting a lot of feedback.

The first video I made was horrible and you can't possibly make a worse video than I started out with. My wife still grimaces at some of my early videos and she still thinks they are funny. She remembers some of them better than I do.

You can easily make a talking head video on something you have and get that up on *YouTube*.

Now it's a lot easier if you do it on a computer because phones often have upload issues. If you can at least make a video on a phone and then get it on a computer to upload it, it's easier. You can also use a camera. Whatever you need to do, this format tends to be the easiest thing to get started.

Note the tendency you have if you are like me to do everything perfect or to try and way overdo it. I did these animated videos before and they took so long to get a 2 minute video done, and they stunk. I was afraid of putting things out there that people wouldn't like.

After getting so much negative feedback at my face, I got to be afraid to show it anymore.

So just put your face out there if you want to get started, and you want it to be as easy as possible. This kind of video is easy if you want to take the next step and you want to be useful, successful and of service to the world.

If you have an *iMac* or an *Apple* computer it's really easy to film talking head videos. I hope this is inspirational for you and that you can get your first video up or the next in this format on *YouTube*.

Screen capture tutorials are the foundation of my success on *YouTube*

Here are the top videos on my *YouTube* channel at www.youtube.com/c/JerryBanfield. Out of the top ten of these, nine are screen capture tutorials and out of the top *20*, almost all of them are screen capture tutorials. They are really powerful because of the global relevance.

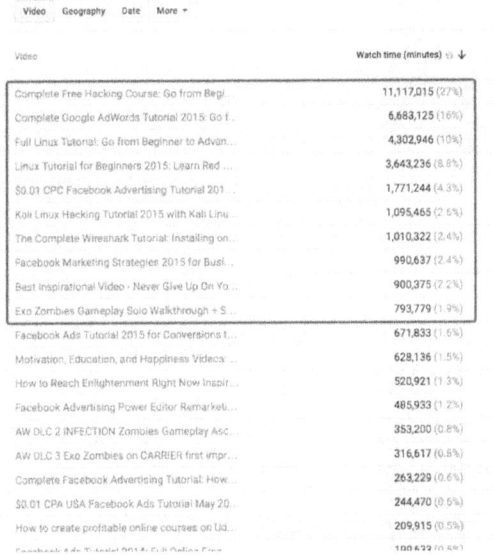

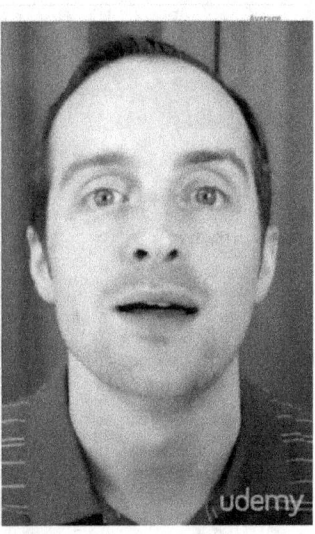

My face is not globally as relevant because people look different, act different, sound different and talk different. Screen capture tutorials work good all over the world because the screen often looks very similar and people want to learn how to do things online.

I'll show you my top videos.

This video below is showing people how to use *Linux* and do ethical hacking online.

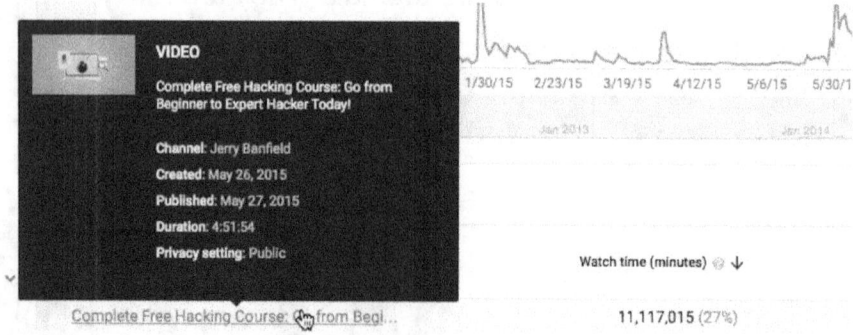

This video is a *Google AdWords* tutorial.

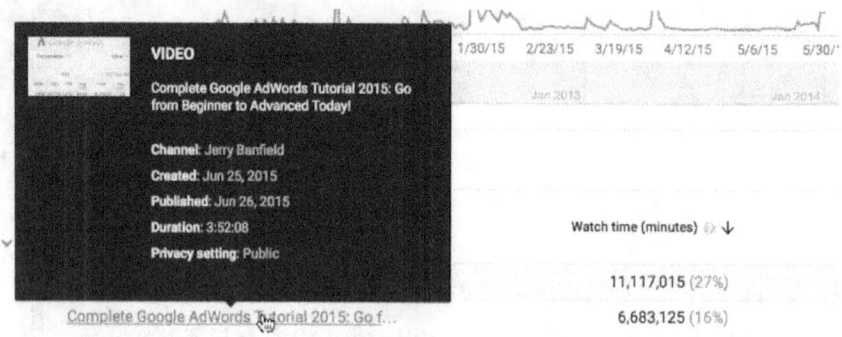

This is a *Linux* tutorial.

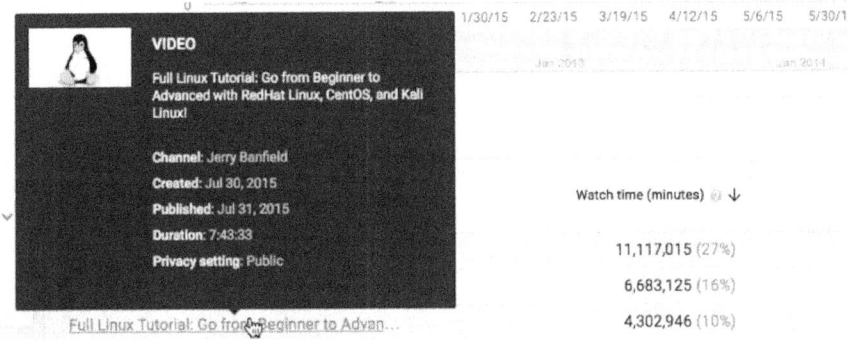

Here is another *Linux* tutorial.

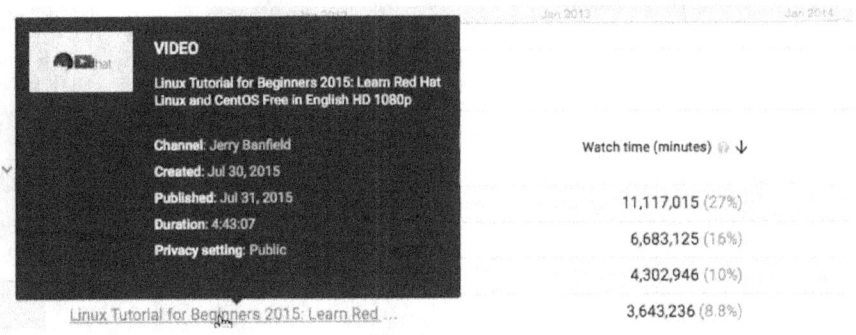

Then I have a *Facebook* ads tutorial, another *Linux* tutorial, a *Wireshark* tutorial, a *Facebook* tutorial and a talking head. Then I have a video game screen capture and finally a *Facebook* ads tutorial again.

Almost all of these are some kind of tutorial showing how to do something. Even if it's playing a video game and showing how to play it successfully. Screen capture tutorials with a nice voiceover are really good on *YouTube* based on the data I'm seeing on my own channel.

You notice that these top screen capture videos have the majority of minutes watched, which is about half of the total minutes watched or more on the channel.

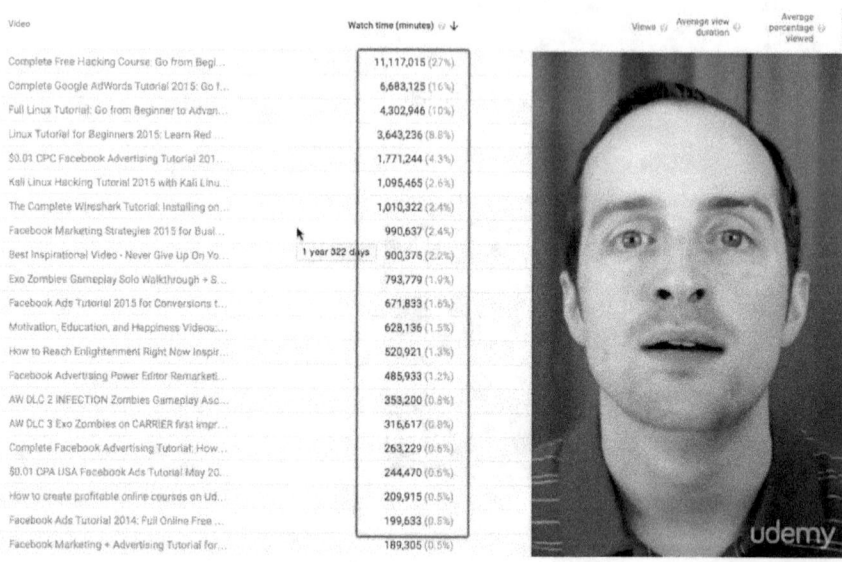

The beauty of it is that you don't have to put your face on camera if you don't want to. These screen capture tutorials have been a miracle for me in everything I've been doing.

When you start, you don't even have to do a good job, if you have a crappy mic or if it doesn't record in the right resolution, it's still better than nothing. My first screen capture tutorial was not good at all compared to the new ones, and yet people loved the original screen capture tutorial I did showing how I was doing my *Facebook* ads.

My first screen capture tutorial took a long time to do, but these new ones I do are so much faster, the audio is better, the screen generally looks better and I can put my face on them.

There are so many different things you can learn to do if you are willing to just start trying to figure out what you can do a screen capture tutorial of and upload it.

You got a great chance to build yourself an impressive freelancing presence online and then, when anyone asks you to do something or wants a proof of your experience, you just hand them the screen capture tutorial. You can say, *"I don't need to tell you about it, I will show you. Take a look at this tutorial and see that I know what to do."*

If you think about putting all of the things you know how to do into little tutorials, you're essentially building a nice portfolio on your *YouTube* channel. Even if only one person watches it that is validation. If you get the right one person to watch it, you can get some amazing things to happen and you might even get millions of people to watch it like I have.

CHAPTER 6

Building a *WordPress* website is the #1 tool for being a successful freelancer

Do you have your self-hosted *WordPress* website set-up? In this chapter I will show you how *WordPress* has helped me and how it can help you too.

I started out with WordPress and am still using it today. The first tool you need to be successful as a freelancer is a *WordPress* website or blog.

Choosing the name of your website is very important and I suggest that you *get a custom URL that never needs to change such as your first and last name*.

The next thing you need is web hosting and after trial and errors, I can tell you that *managed WordPress hosting is the lowest cost and most effective*.

Finally, I want you to *meet the WordPress admin dashboard* from where you can create your unique website or blog.

Read on...

I started out with *WordPress* and am still using it today

A *WordPress* website is the number one tool I think is important for having a successful professional presence online. The reason is that you can put everything that you are doing on your *WordPress* website.

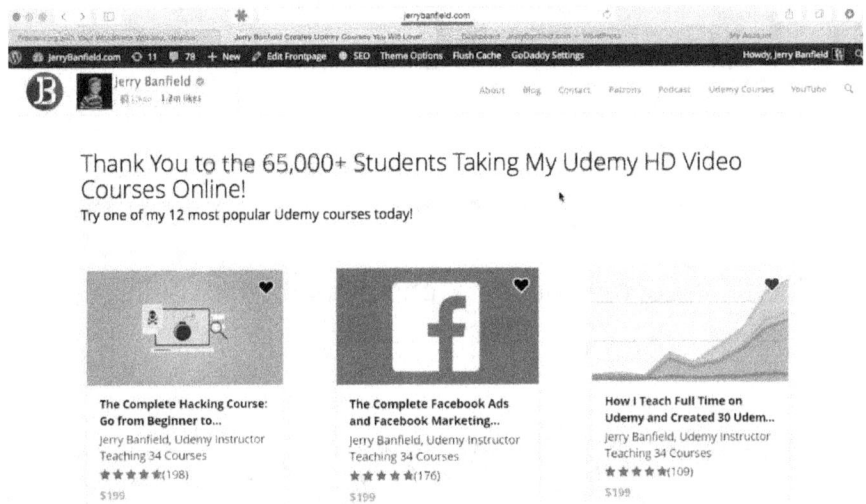

You can use your website to make sales of a product or to convert clients. You can use it to build your attraction, you can attract people to your website and encourage them to take action there.

This is the homepage on my website *JerryBanfield.com* in the image above. You can see that I have my courses for sale first, then I have my blog posts below with my *YouTube* channel.

Then I've got my podcasts, and at the bottom of the website I've got my navigation and links.

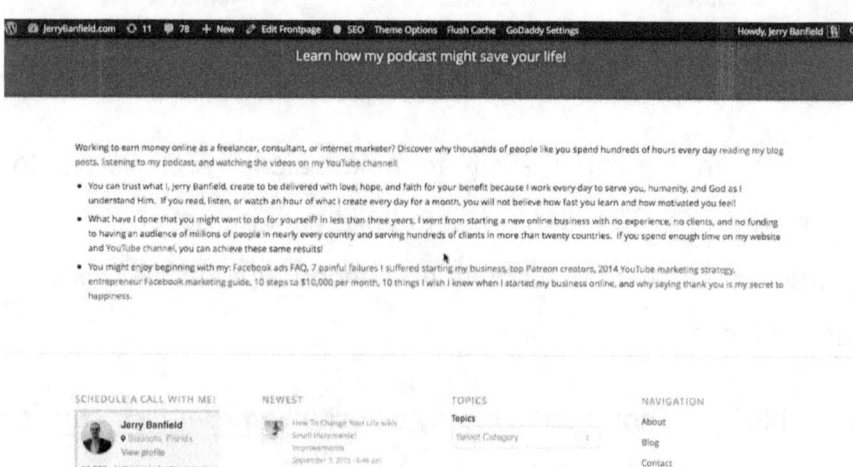

I also have a widget to request a call with me.

Now, at the top of the website, you can see the blog link going to my blog, which is the main function with *WordPress*.

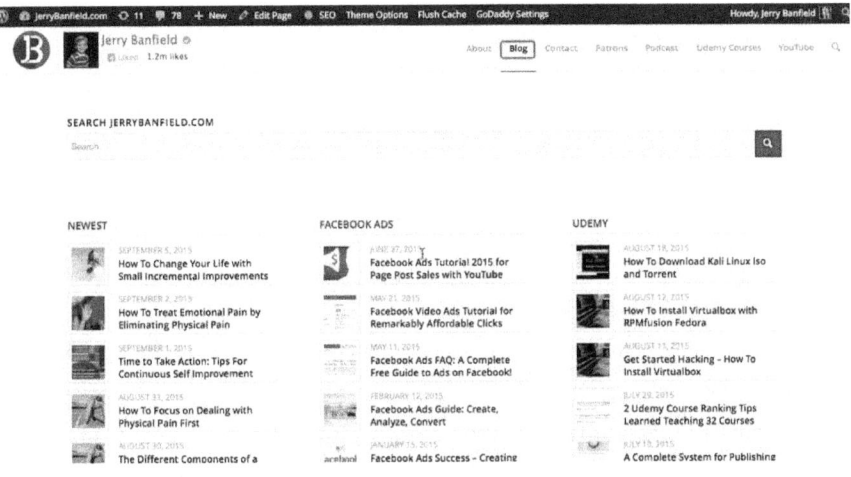

You don't have to have a blog to make a website though, but a blog makes you really look good and it helps out a lot with that love attraction. A blog will help you attract people and give you something to do to build what you are doing.

I like a *YouTube* channel for organic traffic; however, it's often easier to start out and just write blog posts. I've made a lot of different blog posts on my website and it attracts tens of thousands of people a month.

When people come to my website they see something that looks professional and trustworthy. The main thing I like about *WordPress* is both the simplicity and trustworthiness.

You can build a simple website like this with a contact page and everything you want to show. I have a page for my podcasts right there.

Then you can have a sales page like this. Mine brings in the majority of my own promotional sales, which leads to a lot of good things on *Udemy*.

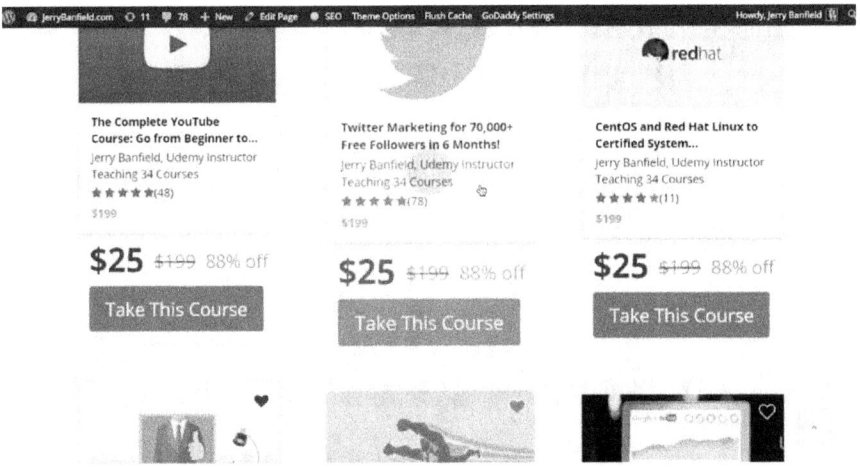

WordPress is where I first started out with and it is still what I'm using today.

Get a custom *URL* that never needs to change such as your first and last name

What you might have noticed on my website is the *URL*: *JerryBanfield.com*.

It's a very nice simple *URL* that never has to change based on what I do. Here is one of the main benefits for it. When you go to *Google* and you search for *Jerry Banfield* what do you see?

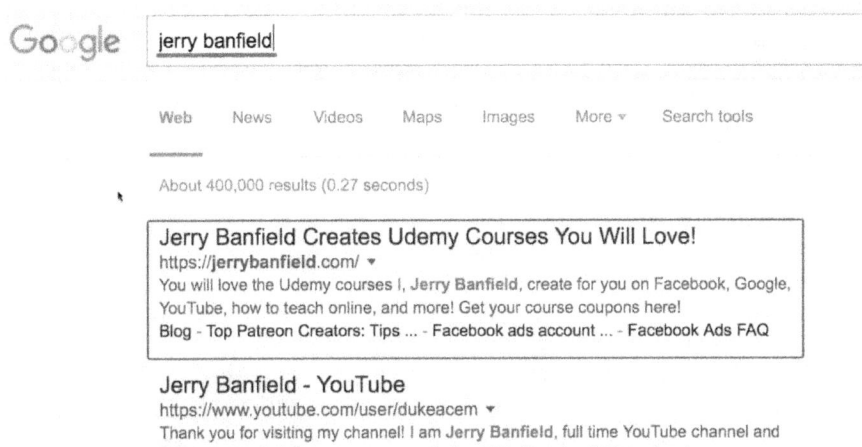

It looks very nice, and professional. The beautiful thing is that it matches my first name and my last name. No matter what I do, *JerryBanfield* stays the same.

You want to be able to have things that stay the same for a website because you don't want to have to make a new one. Here is what I did starting out. I made my website *Banwork.com,* I called my company *Banwork* and I branded everything after *Banwork.com.*

Why BanWork.com For Facebook Page Growth?
banwork.com/ ▼
You will get Facebook likes verified with ads and sponsored stories here! You cannot buy Facebook likes without risking getting your page banned but you can ...

Now it turns out this worked well because of all the things I did wrong, I was able to just sell my website and make a new one. Then you see that the new website I've made works good for *SEO*.

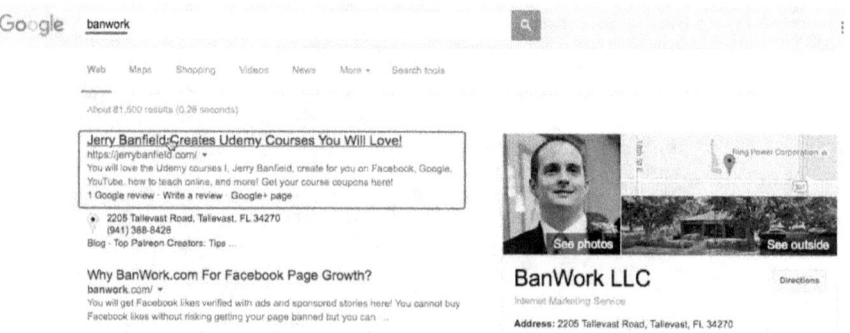

It actually ranks higher on the search for the term "*Banwork*" than the *Banwork* website does itself.

I started out with a company name and I now have *JerryBanfield.com*. I've scrapped and sold *Banwork* because *JerryBanfield.com* is all about me. Whatever I do is on *JerryBanfield.com*.

The main thing I'm doing today is *Udemy* courses, but if I change and start doing *YouTube* or live streaming, or if I change and start giving guitar lessons, whatever I'm doing, *JerryBanfield.com* has that covered.

A custom domain is one of the best things you can do

because it is long term. You can put everything on your domain forever.

Getting a custom domain name is really easy. You just go to some web host like *GoDaddy.com*.

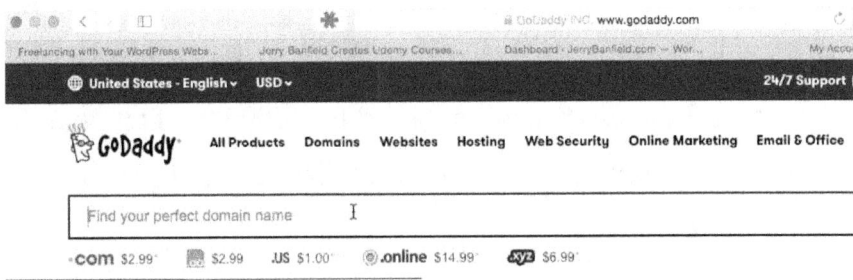

GoDaddy does not compensate me in any way for sharing this, I'm showing it because this is what I use.

You put in your first and last name together as a domain and see if it's taken or not. *JerryBanfield* is obviously taken.

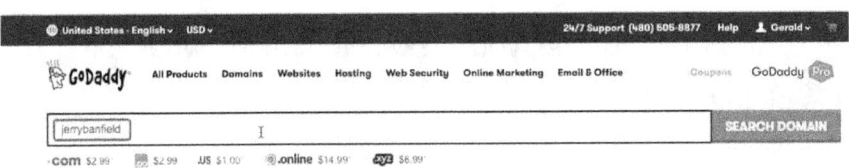

The way I like to do things is with a *.com*. Let's say my name was *GeorgeBanfield*.

georgebanfield		SEARCH AGAIN	CONTINUE TO CART

YES! YOUR DOMAIN IS AVAILABLE. BUY IT BEFORE SOMEONE ELSE DOES.

georgebanfield.com ~~$14.99~~ $2.99*   SELECT
when you register for 2 years or more.
1st year price $2.99 Additional years $14.99

☐ georgebanfield.us Targeting Local shoppers? Add this: $1.00

❶ Get 3 and Save 67% ~~$51.97~~ $17.00*   SELECT
georgebanfield.net
georgebanfield.org
georgebanfield.info

GeorgeBanfield.com is open and for *$2.99* the first year. If I register additional years, I can have *GeorgeBanfield.com* and be there forever.

When I say forever I mean a longtime like for my domain *JerryBanfield.com* which is registered through *18 April 2025*. I'm not planning on going anywhere.

When you are getting started, growing or building for the future, you want to be in one place where you can sit and stay there. If you are trying to freelance, make money online or be an entrepreneur online, you're likely to change what you do lots of times.

I've changed what I do a lot of times.

This is why I have a blog with categories like *Facebook, Udemy, Patreon, YouTube, Google, Digital Marketing, Dating, Online Business, Relationships* and even *Affiliate Marketing* for things I've tried to do.

There are also books I have tried to start writing, tips on making money and on *League of Legends,* and all kinds of random things. They're all on my website.

"Time travel is real" is a story I started writing before.

Time Travel is Real – Go Backwards or Forwards in Time To Appreciate Now

March 6, 2015 / in Digital Marketing, Inspirational / by Jerry Banfield

How many times have you wished you could travel in time? Back in time or forward in time to somewhere besides where you are now? Time travel is real and I will show you exactly how you can travel in time. I will explain it quickly for you in this video. It's amazing and you are about to get the secret for how to travel in time.

I've wanted to travel back into the past a lot in my life. I've looked back and thought "man, I wish I could go back and do that again. I wish I could try and be a better person. I wish I could know what I know now and go back in to the past with that knowledge." Does this sound like a thought you've had before? I know that my mom has expressed this thought to

As you can see I even have *time travel* as a topic on my blog and it gets search results. This is why I have *JerryBanfield.com* because I can put everything all in one spot and as I just showed you with *Google*, it looks really professional when people search for you and your custom *URL* comes up.

One of the things that does not look professional is using a free website like a *WordPress.com* or a *Wix* website. Any website that is free doesn't look professional and it's not even worth starting out on.

I just showed you how you can get a domain probably even cheaper than *$2.99* to get started depending on what host you use. Grab that custom domain in getting started. That's one of the things that you can look a lot more professional and established, at a very small cost. Then from there, you got to figure out hosting.

Managed *WordPress* hosting is the lowest cost and most effective

Once you've got your custom *URL* and you've decided you want to use a self-hosted *WordPress* blog, then the key is to host your website with a hosting company.

The tricks I'll give you in this section can save you a gigantic amount of money, pain and frustration. I've spent more than *$5,000* in a lot of ways and I should not have spent so much on having my website hosted.

I've also spent hundreds of hours with website hosting and it was the main aggravation when I started. In fact, it was so exasperating that I moved over to *Google* sites, which is a nightmare! I would not go back to *WordPress* for two years because of the nightmare the original hosting company posed for me.

I'm going to show you exactly what I'm doing now. What I'm using is called *"managed WordPress hosting."* You can *Google* it to get a look at lots of good options.

Go gle managed wordpress hosting

Web   News   Videos   Images   Sho

About 2,150,000 results (0.32 seconds)

Managed *WordPress* hosting means that the hosting company has setup their servers and programmed everything to function optimally for *WordPress*. This is ideal for cost and for performance because *WordPress* is a pretty low maintenance in terms of what you actually need if everything is setup correctly.

Companies that do *managed WordPress hosting* can afford to host a lot of *WordPress* websites at a good fast speed without needing to dump a bunch of wasted money onto all kinds of servers.

Now, if you just try and go for website hosting generally, you'll often need a lot more performance out of your host than with managed *WordPress* hosting.

Managed WordPress hosting is what I use and it is very easy. Unfortunately, it took me a long time to find it and I am sharing this with you with the hope that you won't have to go through everything I went through.

The first company I hosted with just had a regular kind of website hosting. An absolute nightmare!

I also had *Shared* hosting. Nightmare!

There were porn websites on the same IP address as my website was on, which was bad for search results, bad for user trust if someone really looked into my website and it also went really slow. You want a website that loads fast and *managed WordPress hosting* will usually give you the fastest load time.

What I mean by load time is that you want the time spent downloading a page to be low. I had as much as 7 seconds on my shared hosting before and I paid a hundred of dollars for it. It's about the same cost for *managed WordPress hosting*.

Time spent downloading a page (in milliseconds)

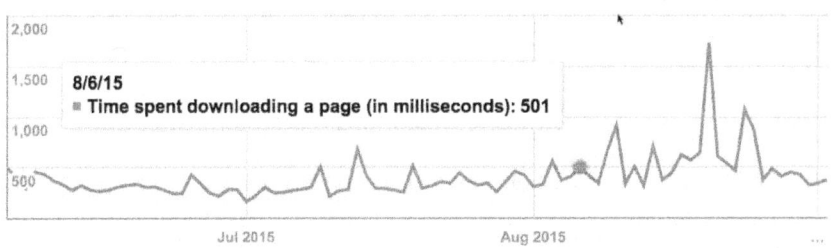

You can see in the image above my consistent low page times. Of course, there's an issue a couple of days, but most of the page load times are pretty low and that means the website comes in at a pretty good speed.

Now, here's which hosting I decided on after googling relentlessly and looking around to find what was the best. I was already registering my domains on *GoDaddy* as I showed you, so I'm hosting my *WordPress* website on *GoDaddy* as well, and it's working very well.

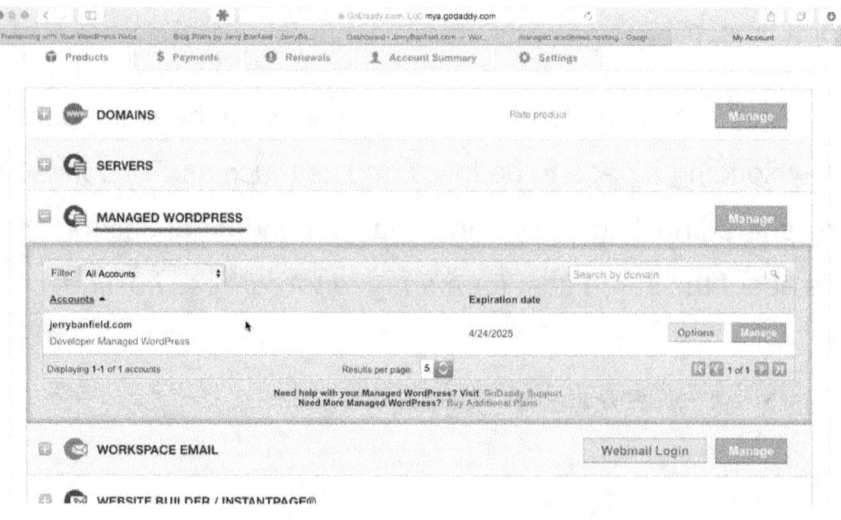

I don't get compensated at all by *GoDaddy* for recommending them, but it's what I use and it works really good. You may go with any company of your choice.

WordPress Engine was another company I considered going with, but *GoDaddy* ended up being cheaper and I already was a customer there.

I was with *HostGator* before for a dedicated server. It worked really good but it was *$4,000* a year, so that's why I switched over to *GoDaddy* managed *WordPress.*

I don't know which company on the market is the best today, but I do know that if you pick any *managed WordPress website hosting*, you are likely to come out pretty well ahead compared to doing anything else.

What you'll notice is that I've got my hosting paid for ten years.

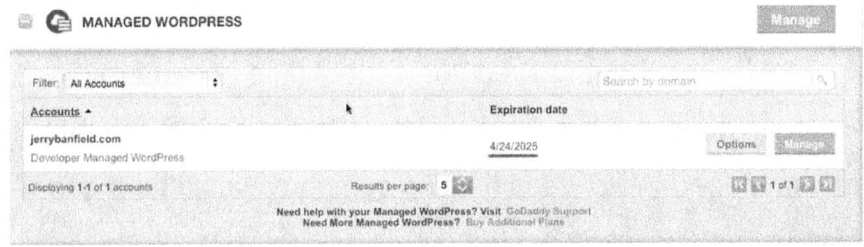

I'm sharing this with you so that you have the option to not struggle and suffer as much as I did. Hosting has been one of the most aggravating parts of my business since the day I started.

This is a *WordPress* admin dashboard with its *GoDaddy* settings and everything is pretty easy to use. I'm sure a lot of other *WordPress* companies that do managed hosting can make it easy for you too!

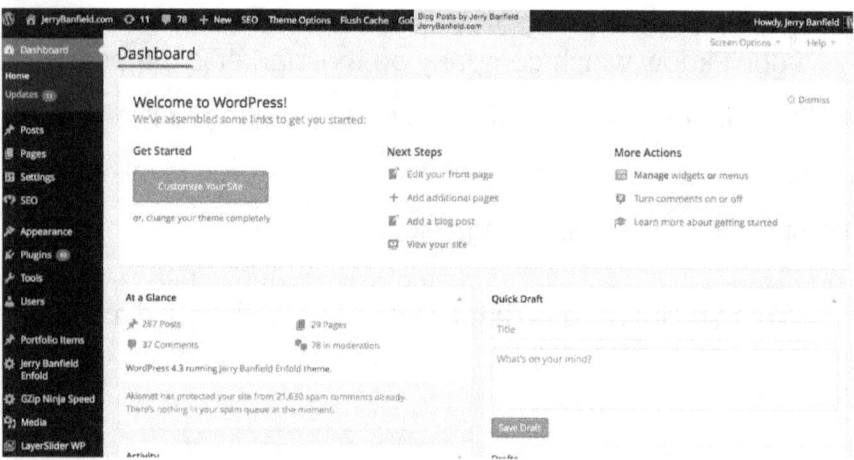

I really hope that I saved you a lot of time and energy in finding a good solution for your *WordPress* hosting and that any *managed WordPress hosting* company would be a good fit to get your website hosted on.

Meet the *WordPress* admin dashboard

Once you have successfully installed *WordPress* with whatever host you are using, then you'll get something like this, which is the *WordPress* admin dashboard.

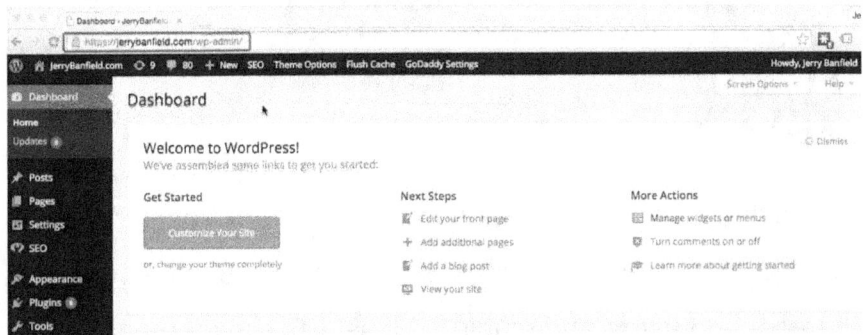

It should be on your website at *URL/wp-admin/*.

This top bar may look a little bit different with your host. You can see that I have this *GoDaddy* settings tab, a *Flush Cache* tab, and since I'm using a theme and plugins, I have some additional options up there that you may or may not have yet.

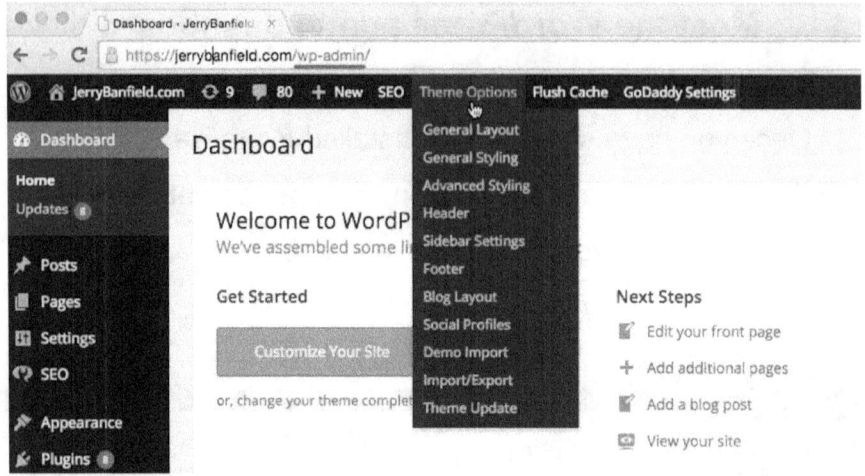

So this is the *Wordpress* admin dashboard from where you run the backend of your website. This is where you setup themes, add users and plugins. Mess with the menu and get your website setup how you want it to.

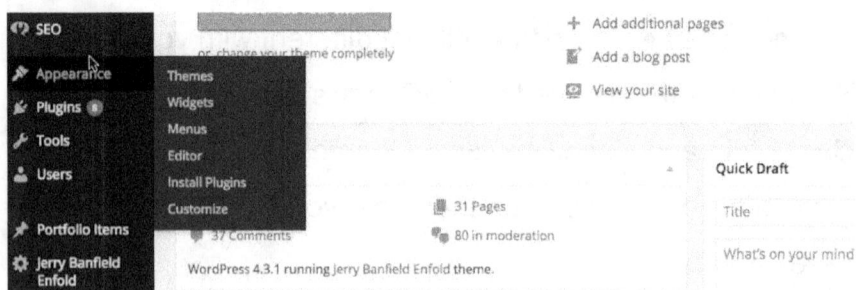

The key thing to note is the theme. You want to be able to use themes with your website and you have the possibility to use the default theme to start with.

The themes are in the *Appearance* section and you can see that I tried a few of them.

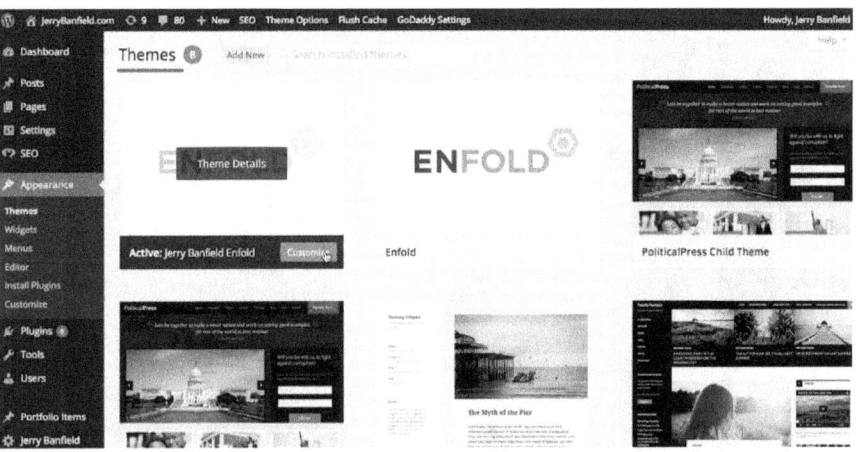

Then, what you do is have the theme you want to use active and it will modify your entire website to a specific design and look.

The time you get your theme right is when you get your website installed because you don't want to change between themes. Once you set everything in your theme, if you change it over to another one it will change everything.

You can look around within *WordPress* and figure out the theme you want. The theme you pick is very important for how your website looks and all the basic functions.

If I show you my theme here in the *WordPress* admin dashboard, you'll notice all kinds of options.

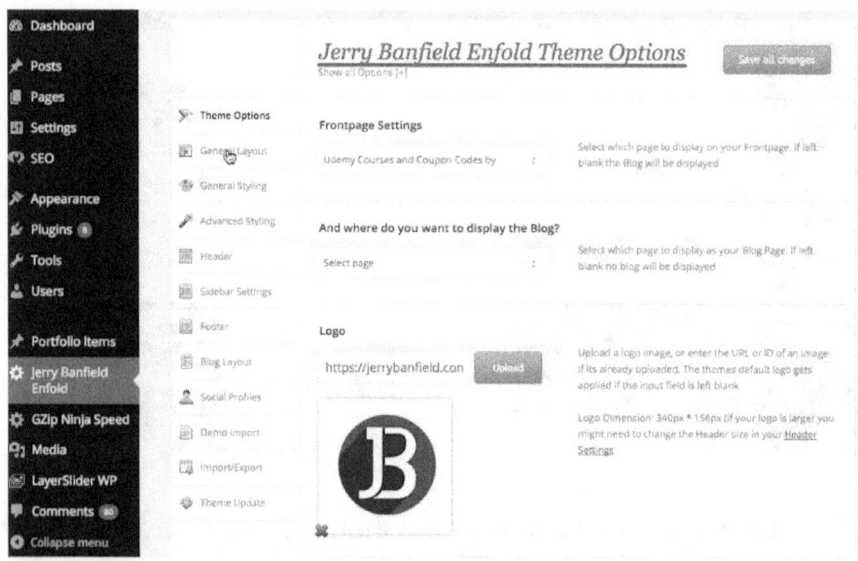

The layout, the styling, the header, the sidebar, the footer, the blog layout and all kinds of things are setup by the theme. So the theme is the single biggest decision you make with your *WordPress* website.

Try out as many themes as you want right when you get your website started and once you have figured out which one you want, then you can go from there.

CHAPTER 7

Get started with *Upwork*: the world's largest online freelancing platform

If you are getting started online and don't know where to go, I have good news for you in this chapter.

What is Upwork and how can you use it? Upwork is the largest online work platform in the world and there are some amazing things you can do.

I will show you *what I am doing on Upwork today and what opportunities you might have*.

You might not be sure of what skills you have that people need and *Upwork is a good place to get to know the talents you have*, even if you don't get hired.

Getting your first job is the most difficult and *if you want to get hired on Upwork, put time and effort into your profile*, and build your portfolio. Clients do not want to hire people who show nothing.

Read on…

What is *Upwork* and how can you use it?

Upwork is the largest online work platform in the world and there are some amazing things you can do. The main functionality as you can see is right here to find freelancers, or to become your own freelancer and to get found.

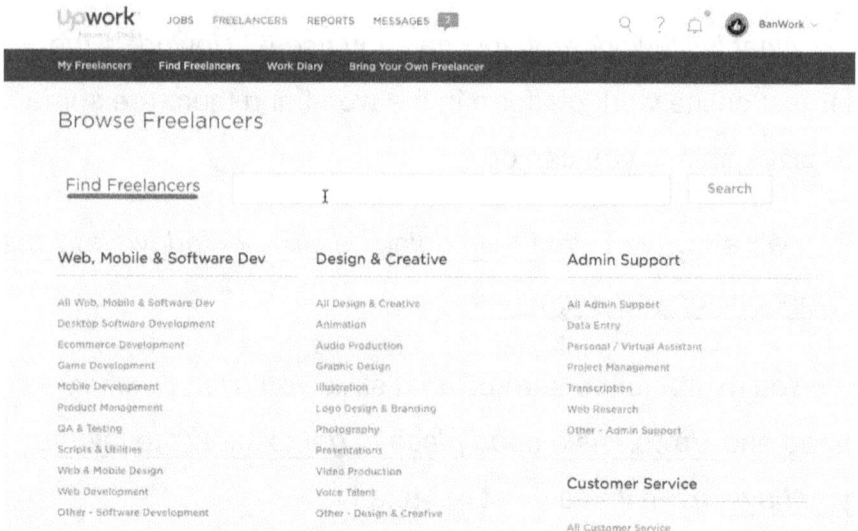

This is a main thing I use *Upwork* for and here's an example of what takes place on this website.

This is the job I have up now: *"YouTube Video Content Writer."*

This is something I'm hiring for, with a thousand dollar

budget on the job posting.

It's an indefinite job because I'm continuing making *YouTube* videos and I will need more of the same work done. Then, below the job description is how many people have made proposals. One will be interviewed, hired and get paid.

The beauty of it is that everything is done online so you can do the work anywhere in the world. *Upwork* is an amazing platform where you can use your skills to make some real money online.

This is what I'm doing on *Upwork*, I'm hiring people now.

As a person who hires a lot of people on *Upwork* and who's work with hundreds of different people, you might appreciate learning about some of the things that I see make it easy to be a successful freelancer, and make it easy to hire people successfully on *Upwork*.

I've spent over *$30,000* on paying people to work from the comfort of their home, to do things for me from all over the world in all kinds of different countries.

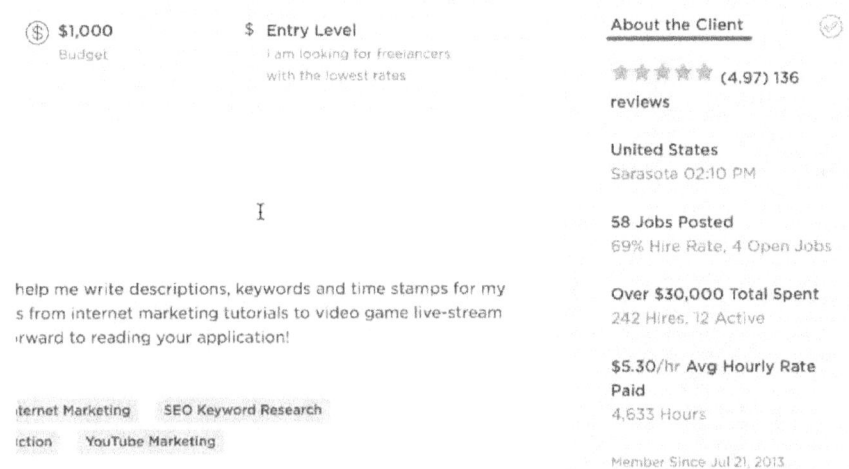

Now, *$5.30* is the average hourly rate I've paid. However, if you look at the numbers above, a significant part of what I've paid has been project based jobs.

This is what you can do on *Upwork* and it's a question of how much effort you want to put into it learning about what goes on, and what the easiest opportunities are for you to be successful.

What I am doing on *Upwork* today and what opportunities you might have

This *"YouTube Video Content Writer"* job post is a perfect example of a great way you can get started.

I don't mean with this actual job post, but with this type of job post on *Upwork*. If you're looking to hire, this is one of the most valuable things I think *Upwork* offers, and it is the ability to find people that would do time consuming tasks well, and completely handled and outsourced.

What this job post looks for is someone to take the *YouTube* video below and write a description.

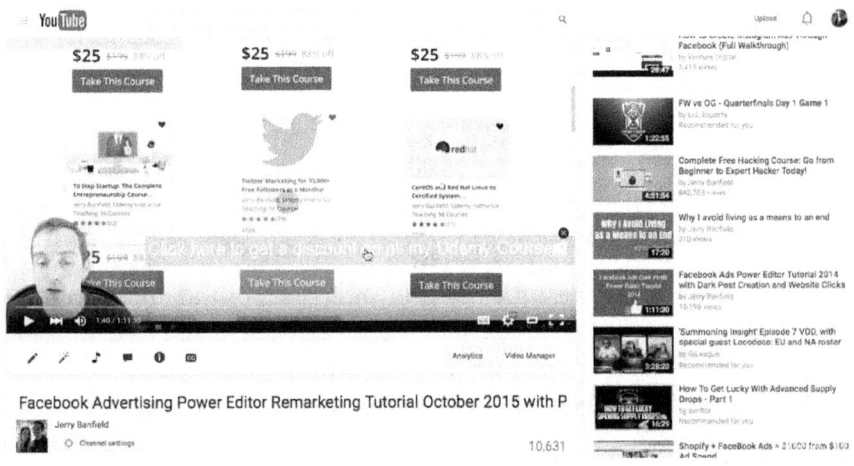

This is a finished work below and this is how it looks like.

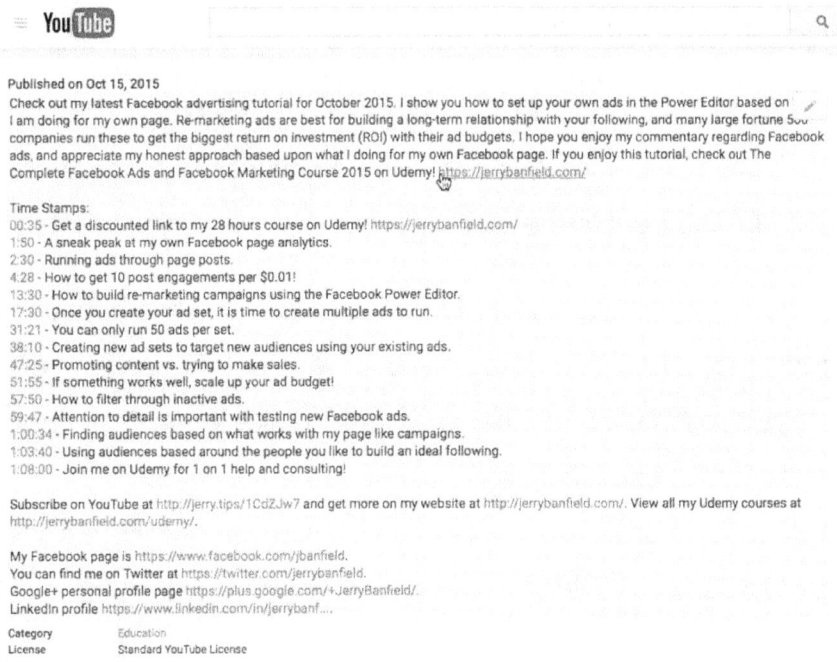

Published on Oct 15, 2015

Check out my latest Facebook advertising tutorial for October 2015. I show you how to set up your own ads in the Power Editor based on I am doing for my own page. Re-marketing ads are best for building a long-term relationship with your following, and many large fortune 500 companies run these to get the biggest return on investment (ROI) with their ad budgets. I hope you enjoy my commentary regarding Facebook ads, and appreciate my honest approach based upon what I doing for my own Facebook page. If you enjoy this tutorial, check out The Complete Facebook Ads and Facebook Marketing Course 2015 on Udemy! https://jerrybanfield.com/

Time Stamps:
00:35 - Get a discounted link to my 28 hours course on Udemy! https://jerrybanfield.com/
1:50 - A sneak peak at my own Facebook page analytics.
2:30 - Running ads through page posts.
4:28 - How to get 10 post engagements per $0.01!
13:30 - How to build re-marketing campaigns using the Facebook Power Editor.
17:30 - Once you create your ad set, it is time to create multiple ads to run.
31:21 - You can only run 50 ads per set.
38:10 - Creating new ad sets to target new audiences using your existing ads.
47:25 - Promoting content vs. trying to make sales.
51:55 - If something works well, scale up your ad budget!
57:50 - How to filter through inactive ads.
59:47 - Attention to detail is important with testing new Facebook ads.
1:00:34 - Finding audiences based on what works with my page like campaigns.
1:03:40 - Using audiences based around the people you like to build an ideal following.
1:08:00 - Join me on Udemy for 1 on 1 help and consulting!

Subscribe on YouTube at http://jerry.tips/1CdZJw7 and get more on my website at http://jerrybanfield.com/. View all my Udemy courses at http://jerrybanfield.com/udemy/.

My Facebook page is https://www.facebook.com/jbanfield.
You can find me on Twitter at https://twitter.com/jerrybanfield.
Google+ personal profile page https://plus.google.com/+JerryBanfield/.
LinkedIn profile https://www.linkedin.com/in/jerrybanf....

Category   Education
License   Standard YouTube License

Someone has watched the video and written this description out.

This doesn't take very long to do and I could do it myself, but it takes me long enough to do that it actually discourages me from making more videos, just because of the description I have to write. One of the biggest difference between videos that get watched more and videos that don't, is a nice description.

There are all kinds of jobs like these on *Upwork* and as you can see, all the person needs to do is watch the video, and then type a description up. If you've completed a few grades in school, this is something that is possible.

There are tons of jobs like these on *Upwork* and there are tons of good people that can help out doing work for clients.

So, why do I say this is a great way to start? It is because there's not a lot of skills you need to have or emphasize. You just need to actually do the work for jobs like these. You can do the work, learn and earn. As you learn and watch videos on how to do some kind of work, then you can get more skills that will be more valuable and paid at a higher rate.

Work is also project based and you can see below that I ask what they charge per video. This way, I know what I'm getting and whoever does the work knows that they're getting a flat payment for a certain amount of work.

You will be asked to answer the following questions when submitting a proposal:
1. What past project or job have you had that is most like this one and why?

2. Are you a native English speaker?

3. What will you charge per video?

These kinds of jobs are awesome on *Upwork* because they don't require you to have a bunch of technical knowledge, which you might or might not have starting out. Now the best opportunities on *Upwork* are the ones that require specialized knowledge.

The other jobs I'm hiring need a lot more specialized knowledge. I'm looking for contractors that have programming experience.

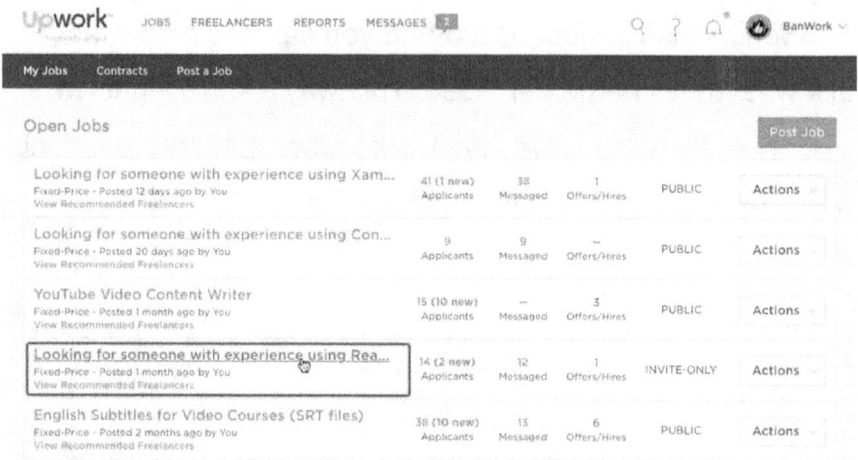

The job offer above is for a *React.js* course. I'm looking for contractors who have programming experience, specifically in *React.js*. You'll notice that this is a *$5,000* budget to make video tutorials.

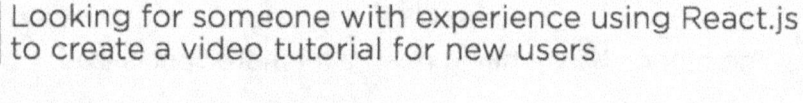

You can see below that I am willing to pay *$50* per video. You can often be paid really well to teach and do technical experience jobs on *Upwork*.

Details

I am looking for a professional with experience using React JavaScript to create a video tutorial for new users. The tutorial will consist primarily of screen capture and voice over explaining what you are doing. I would like you to begin with the basics, and move on to applications or even a project. Ideally I would like videos to be anywhere from 8-12 minutes in length and I would like to pay $50 per video. I need someone that speaks fluent English. Thank you for taking the time to view my post and I look forward to hearing from you!

Start with something that uses a skill you already have, and you can continue to level up and develop your skills while working on *Upwork*. Then, you can get the higher paying jobs.

Now, if you already have these skills, go straight for them. If you don't, getting these easy jobs on *Upwork* that just require you to use the skills you do have will give you time to learn into these more higher paying skills.

So this is how I am using *Upwork* and this is an opportunity I see available for you.

Upwork is a good place to get to know the talents you have

When you have to enter your skills in an online profile, it's a great opportunity to get to know yourself better.

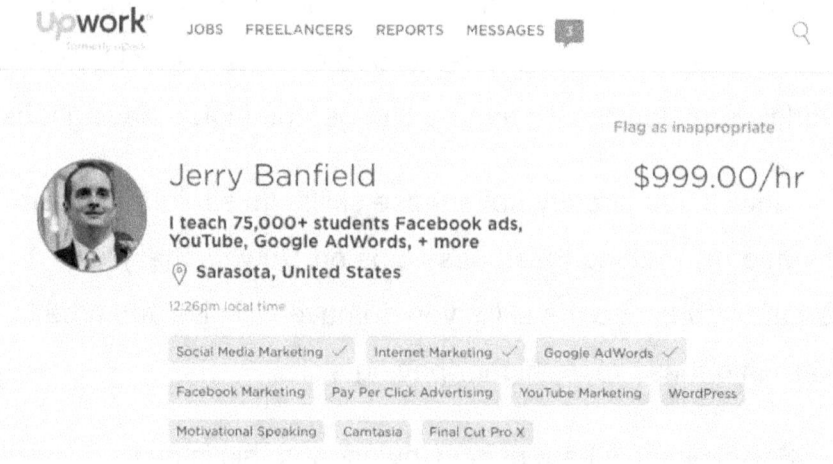

Ultimately, if you want to work online successfully as a freelancer, you want to be able to know the skills you have in a way that you can clearly describe them to someone else.

Below is my *Upwork* personal profile where I show what I do and you'll see that I've listed my skills, then I show proof that I actually know how to do them on my *Udemy* page, my website and my *YouTube* channel.

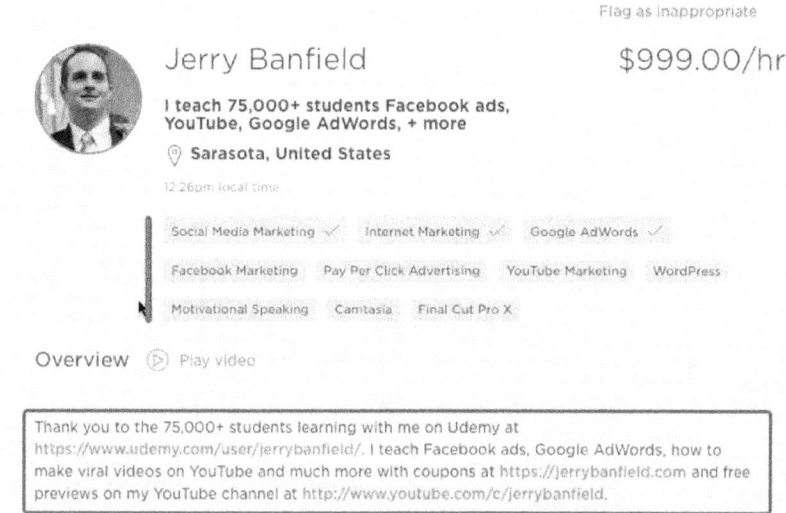

Then I put up a couple of things to show what I've done with those skills.

Your *Upwork* profile is like a résumé and a portfolio that you can use online. Just the work of building that résumé or that portfolio helps you get to know yourself better, and then through getting to know yourself better, you can more effectively match what skills you have with what work people need to be done. That's where you end up making money.

What I'm lucky to have been able to do is to match my skills up with what people need. *Upwork* is really helpful to figure out what it is people need and where you meet up with that.

What you can see on my profile, below the headline, is my best opportunity to show what skills I have in terms of search results.

When someone is viewing my profile, they can see a lot more in the portfolio, which is a great place to show and not tell.

When I say I do *Facebook*, I have a link to my *Facebook* page. When I say I do *YouTube*, I have a link to my *YouTube* channel, both with pictures of what I've done.

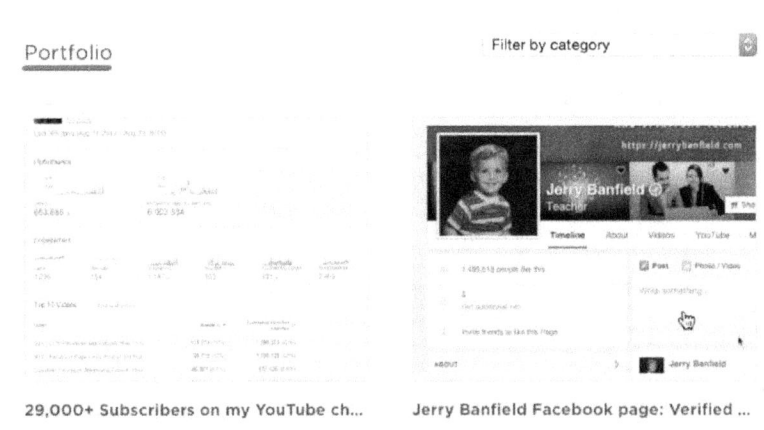

29,000+ Subscribers on my YouTube ch...   Jerry Banfield Facebook page: Verified ...

The *Tests* are below the *Portfolio* section. Now, I haven't taken these tests for a couple of years, but when I took them I got good scores. The tests are a good way to really see what skills you have.

Tests

Name	Score (out of 5)		Time to Complete	
Internet Marketing Test	4.75	Top 10%	14 mins	Details
Analytical Skills Test	4.25	Top 10%	45 mins	Details

Now, what does a good score in the *Google AdWords* test really mean if you can't get conversions or actually do good work. It doesn't matter how good you can do with the test, you have to get the skills too.

Even if you never get hired on *Upwork*, I hope you can see the value of going through and taking time in cataloging all of these skills you have, so that you can understand what you do.

If you want to get hired on *Upwork*, put time and effort into your profile

The biggest weakness I see most people who want to get hired as freelancer have, is a profile that they clearly haven't spent much time working on. You have to put some time and energy into making a good profile if you want to get hired on *Upwork*.

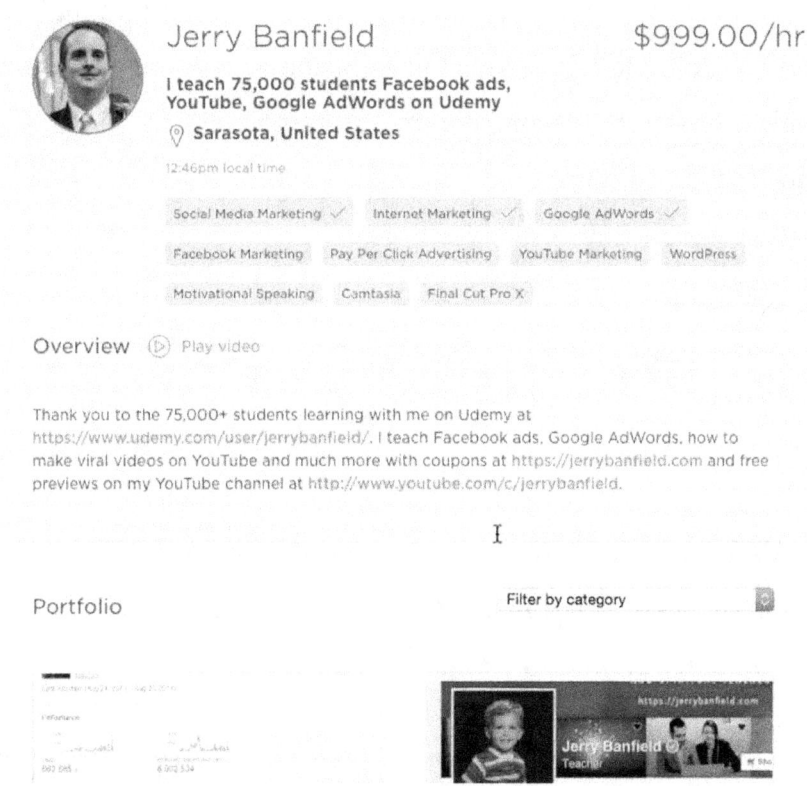

You need maybe an hour or so of basic time to just put in a

headline and a few skills, and then there's a bit more work in writing about what you can do and make your portfolio.

It's very hard to get that first job or two and if you want to get hired, the one way you can really stand out is just to take the time to make your profile look good. Do your best to get a good picture, to get everything lined up and to show rather than tell.

In the overview, the client doesn't need to read about how you are going to make their life amazing and do all this great work. Write a short overview and preferably link to things you've actually done.

Overview ⓟ Play video

Thank you to the 75,000+ students learning with me on Udemy at
https://www.udemy.com/user/jerrybanfield/. I teach Facebook ads, Google AdWords, how to make viral videos on YouTube and much more with coupons at https://jerrybanfield.com and free previews on my YouTube channel at http://www.youtube.com/c/jerrybanfield.

Whatever skills you are using, if you have a *YouTube* video showing how you do that skill, it's so much more powerful than trying to explain it in an overview.

The portfolio is where you shine. If you say you do graphic design, show the graphics you've made. If you say you do *WordPress* writing, show some of the blog posts you've written or some of the work you've done for clients.

If you say you do *Social Media Marketing* like I do, for Heaven's sake put some pictures in of pages you have promoted. If you say you do *YouTube*, show some results on your *YouTube* channel.

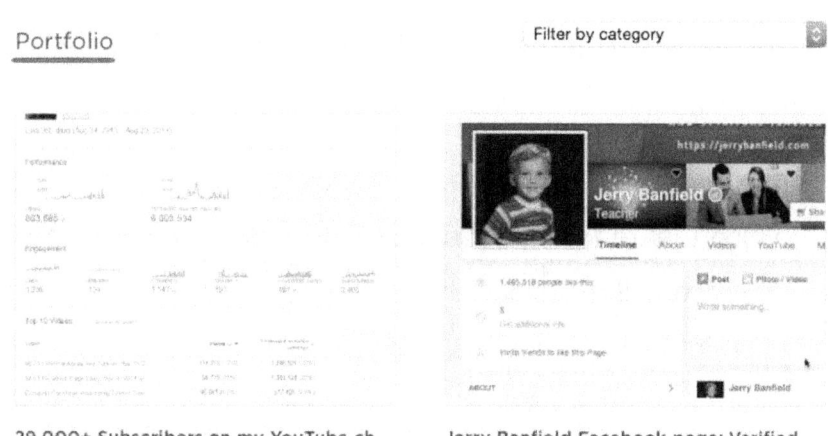

29,000+ Subscribers on my YouTube ch...   Jerry Banfield Facebook page: Verified ...

If you say you can do *Internet Marketing*, then take *15* minutes to do the test. You should take the test for every skill you say you have.

Tests

Name	Score (out of 5)		Time to Complete	
Internet Marketing Test	4.75	Top 10%	14 mins	Details
Analytical Skills Test	4.25	Top 10%	45 mins	Details

These tests took hours to complete and they are the ones I'm showing on my profile because I got my best scores on them.

Take the time to fill out a real employment history, not just something that reads like a résumé and write something that has more life to it. Put your education in and put some time and effort into your *Upwork* profile.

Even if you don't get hired, you'll learn more about what you need to do in order to advance yourself online. When you realize you don't have any good videos, or you don't have any good things to show for what you are trying to do, then you can see the work you can do in order to make a good portfolio.

When you start and you don't have much to do, it's a great opportunity to show what you can do and take time to build that portfolio, or your own website, and to make some videos on *YouTube* or whatever it is you need to do. Clients don't want to hire people who haven't done anything or who haven't shown they've done something.

If you don't have anything to show, take the time making it. Your *Upwork* profile is a great place to get motivated to show what you can do, and the more you show, the more you stand out from everyone else.

Almost everyone else just tells you what they can do. If you can show what you can do, you don't have to explain much. As you can see my profile is very short, I don't need to write what I can do because I've got my *Udemy* profile, my website and *YouTube* channel, and these portfolios. I don't need to sit and explain it for 6 hours, you can see exactly what I've already done.

I hope this motivates you to put that work into your profile before you go to apply in a whole bunch of jobs. You can waste your time a lot applying to jobs if you don't have a profile that looks good.

If you see your profile just doesn't have what it takes to be good right now, work on that before trying to get a job. That can save you a ton of time and energy down the road if you put the energy up front into presenting yourself well.

CHAPTER 8

Fiverr is the easiest place to make your first *$20* online

If you want to get started as a freelancer online, I will show you in this chapter that *Fiverr* is probably the easiest place. _What is Fiverr and what can you do with it?_

What am I doing today on Fiverr and what opportunities might you have? I was ordered *82* gigs on *Fiverr* without much effort and I've ordered *648* gigs that have been completed.

The 80/20 principle on Fiverr for power buyers and power sellers will make you understand what you need to do to be successful on *Fiverr*.

Finally, you should _buy and sell on Fiverr for maximum learning and earning_. Being a buyer will help you understand the process and help you be a better seller, and being a seller will help you be a better buyer.

Read on...

Jerry Banfield & Michel Gerard

What is *Fiverr* and what can you do with it?

If you want to make your first *$5*, *$20* or *$100* online, I believe *Fiverr* is the easiest place to do that. If you need some simple things done to support what you are doing in your business, *Fiverr* is also the easiest place to go to.

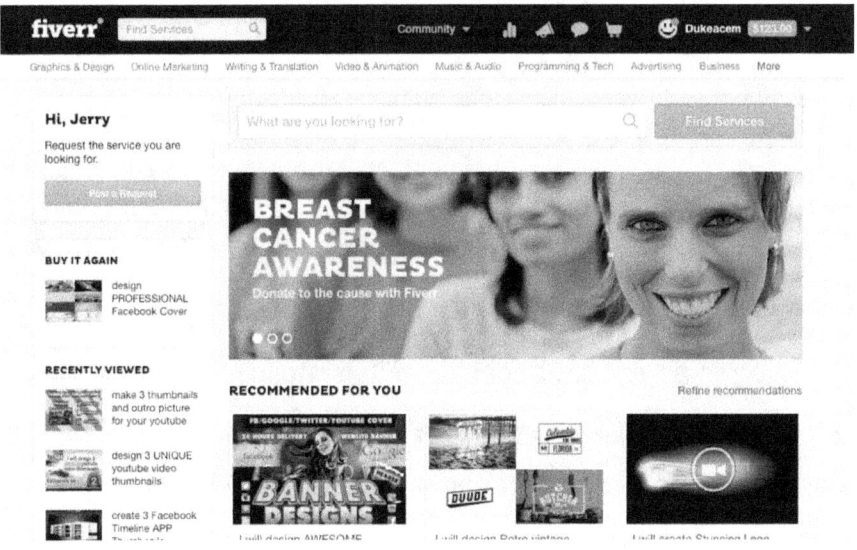

The reason *Fiverr* works good is because it is setup with a simple idea in mind which is executed well. You post a gig or service you are offering to do for *$5* and it's that simple.

If you want a logo done, you type in *"logo"* in the search bar and the next set of search results that come up are all these people who are offering to do a logo for *$5*.

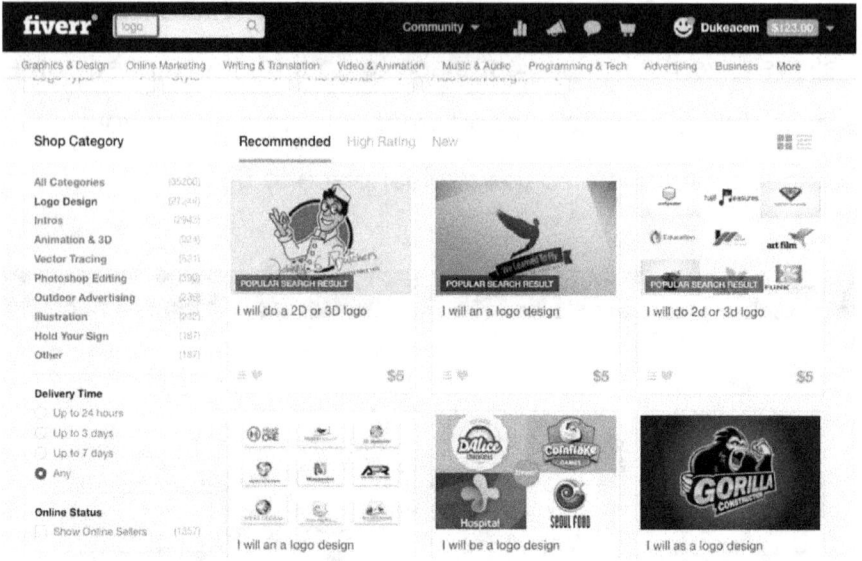

Fiverr is awesome because of its simplicity, you just pick one of these for *$5* and you'll get a logo back. You might not want to design a logo yourself and there are *27,000* people that are willing to do it for *$5*.

There is a lot of opportunities for someone who needs professional services on *Fiverr* to buy them and there is a lot of opportunities to offer something on *Fiverr* that other people are currently doing.

Fiverr was the key to starting my business online. I offered services for a higher price and then bought them on *Fiverr*, that's the first thing I did that made good money.

Fiverr is great for offering anything till you get your business started and then take it to the next level. I am still using *Fiverr* today and I have made hundreds of dollars on *Fiverr* also with very little effort. I'll go through and show you what you can do to make money and to get help doing what you're doing today.

What am I doing today on *Fiverr* and what opportunities might you have?

The main thing I do is buy on *Fiverr*. The important thing to note from that is that there are people like me everywhere around the world who are consistently buying on *Fiverr*.

There's a lot of demand and I think it is important to show you what I am actually doing today on *Fiverr* to validate that I'm here writing this chapter and that it's worth using.

I've ordered *648* gigs that have been completed on *Fiverr*.

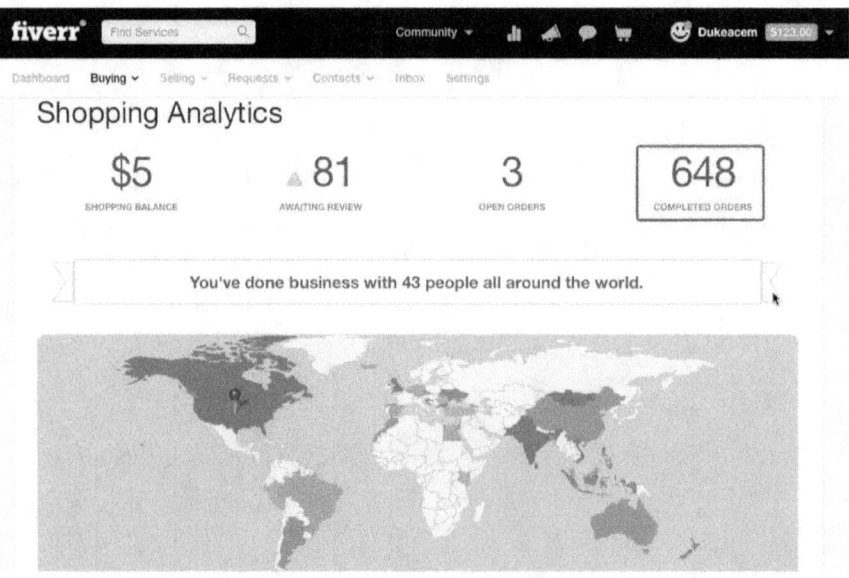

Even though the base price is *$5*, I've spent an average of

$8 or $9 per gig because a lot of gigs had up-sells. I've spent more than $5,000 on *Fiverr* in total and I'm still using it today.

What I have right now are three open orders for thumbnails. Thumbnails are something I need continually as I'm making new videos all the time. It's so much easier to just get someone make a nice thumbnail for $5 instead of fooling around with it myself.

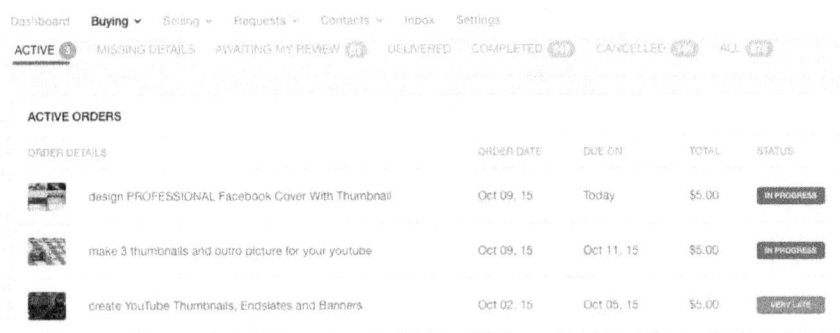

My vice president and co-instructor *Joseph* actually goes and makes the orders for me and interacts on *Fiverr*. What you can see is that I'm consistently using *Fiverr* each day and have no plans to stop using it indefinitely. *Fiverr* is here to stay and grow.

You'll notice that I have a lot of gigs I've ordered that have been cancelled and this happens when the person doing the gig can't fulfill the order. There's a lot of opportunity to offer gigs on *Fiverr* that you can get customers for fairly quickly and this can help you get started.

If you look at my selling on *Fiverr*, I've actually had *82* orders created with me and I've earned *$336* since joining. I've made almost no effort at all to earn that money on *Fiverr*.

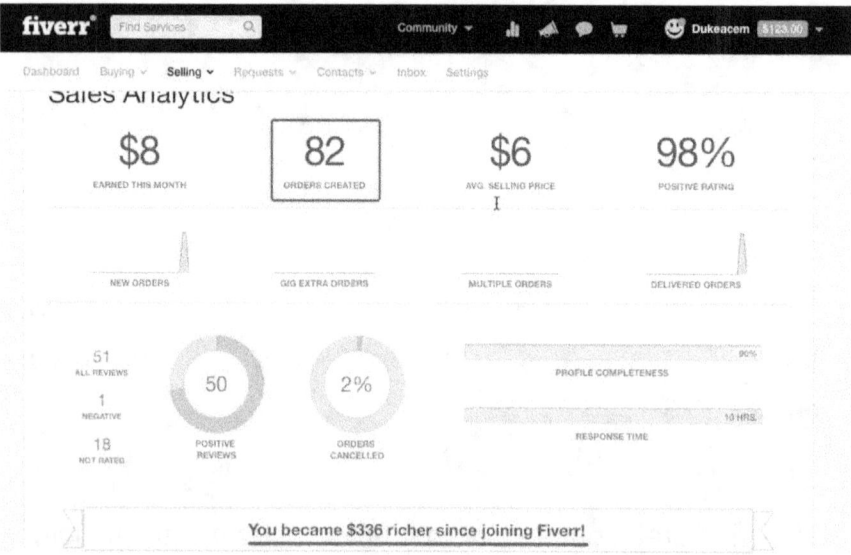

I've made very little effort to promote my gigs and yet I've got people from different countries all over the world ordering from me. I have not done much money as a seller because I have used *Fiverr* more as a buyer to support my business.

If I've earned *$336* without even trying much on *Fiverr*, I'm confident that you can earn a lot more money if you put the effort. I hope this is useful and inspiring for you in your ongoing journey to freelancing online.

The 80/20 principle on *Fiverr* for power buyers and power sellers

The 80/20 *Pareto* principle is very important for *Fiverr* to help you understand where your opportunities are. The 80/20 or *Pareto* principle is referenced to widely in things dealing with economics, wealth and all parts of life.

The basic premise is that there's disproportionate rules in life based on positive reinforcement. Things like 80% of the people in the world have 20% of the wealth while 20% of the people in the world have 80% of the wealth.

Now, actually that's just a rough estimation and often things like wealth get even more skewed like 5% of people in the world hold 95% of the wealth and the other 95% hold 5%. These things happen because of positive reinforcement loops and because people repeatedly do the same things.

Let's see how this works for *Fiverr:*

Around 20% of the buyers will make 80% of the gig purchases.

80% of the people buying on *Fiverr* will only buy 20% of the gigs.

That's a rough estimate because it could be like 90/10 or 70/30. The more skewed it is, and the more important it is whether you are buying or selling.

In both cases it's more important to aim at those power users whether you're on either side. If you are the buyer you often realize that you are likely to interact with other power sellers. You're likely to do business with other sellers who are working a lot on *Fiverr*.

So the opportunity with that is to order from the people who aren't ordered from as often because you can find a real good value out of that. At the same time, it is easier to order from people who are established and who are doing consistently good work on *Fiverr*.

So as a buyer, I know to look outside of the people who are already receiving the most orders.

On any website like *Fiverr*, there tends to be a small percentage of buyers and sellers who get all of the activity, while almost everyone else does nothing. So if you want to use *Fiverr* successfully as a buyer or seller, understanding that is very helpful to get started.

Now what does that mean for you?

If you can start with this in mind, whether you are buying or selling, you can get way ahead and make things easier for you. Life for me has been pretty easy on *Fiverr* as a buyer because I usually order from the same people over and over again. Around half of my orders are from the same small group of people.

You'll notice this principle right below as you can see that over half of my orders are from one country, the USA.

Shopping Analytics

$5	⚠ 81	3	648
SHOPPING BALANCE	AWAITING REVIEW	OPEN ORDERS	COMPLETED ORDERS

You've done business with 43 people all around the world.

371 ORDERS FROM UNITED STATES

What country you're in definitely impacts your ability to be able to make sales or will impact your buying decisions.

If you want to be a seller you've got to aim for that power seller category right from the beginning. It doesn't mean you have to get there from the beginning, it means you want to aim for it because you are not likely to do much otherwise, although I made *$300* without being a power seller.

If you really want to make something out of *Fiverr* as a seller, understand that you will have to end up in that power seller category at some point and that you can see from all the power buyers like me, there's a lot of opportunities there.

I hope this is useful for you in looking at the 80/20 principle for *Fiverr* and that this will allow you to see where the opportunities are, whether you're a buyer or a seller.

Buy and sell on *Fiverr* for maximum learning and earning

For anything you are doing online, here is a simple idea that has helped me a lot. If you want to be a good buyer, it helps to be a seller too. If you want to be a good seller, it helps to be a buyer too.

In other words, if you want to make money on *Fiverr*, you also should be willing to buy gigs. In fact, if you want to sell gigs on *Fiverr*, the first step you can take that might be really helpful is to buy gigs from other people. If you want to buy gigs and use them for your business, it can help you a lot to offer a few gigs for sale and understand what it is like to be a seller.

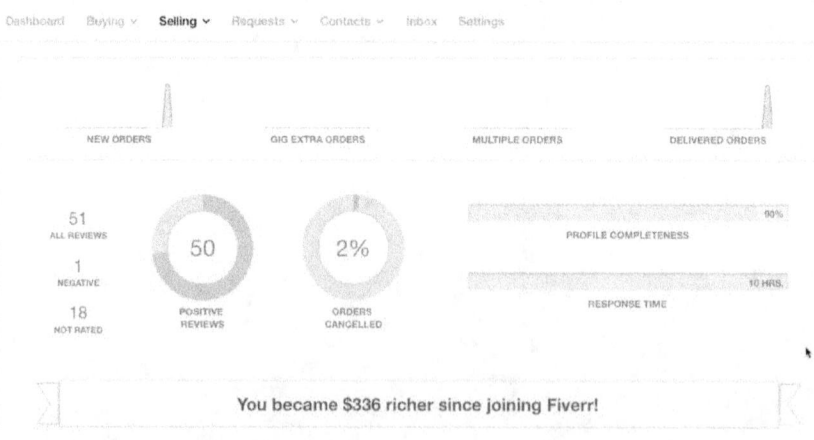

It was useful for me as a buyer to offer my gigs for sale and understand how it is like to deliver a gig for someone, to offer to do something for *$5* and to actually get *$4* out of it. I also learned that everything should be fairly simple and straightforward.

It gave me the opportunity to understand that I should have gratitude for anyone who do work for me for *$4* and not hassle them or give them a hard time. As a seller I know when I'm getting *$4* for something, it's nice not to get wrangled around and have a bunch of problems over this small amount.

Learning as a seller on *Fiverr* helped me to be a better buyer. I know that for *$5*, all I am going to get is something that's done very quickly and I shouldn't expect a lot out of the seller. If I order a bigger gig and get some extras then I expect a bit more.

Doing both the buying and the selling on *Fiverr* gives you this visceral level of understanding about how things work that will help you do much better at whatever it is you are trying to do.

As a seller, I understand that what I'm willing to put into is a big part of the equation, and as a buyer it's often better to give a lot of people a chance at $5 and see who is really willing to do the most.

If you buy and sell gigs on *Fiverr*, you can count on a lot better experience as either a buyer or a seller. If you want to sell, buy gigs first. If you want to buy, you could probably go straight into buying.

If you want to sell, absolutely buy 3 or 5 gigs from other people so that you can learn the buying process and you'll know it from the point of view of the seller.

CHAPTER 9

Managing relationships with clients and customers successfully

In this chapter I am going to show you that _having clients and customers is like dating. You both need to get what you need_.

If you think that having hundreds of clients is the best way to go, then see that for me _fewer clients that love you is better than a lot of clients that like you_.

Getting started as a freelancer is challenging, but know that _going from zero to one client is the biggest difference_. Then, you can go from one to two, two to three, three to four, etc…

Scaling, scaling and scaling!

Forget scaling until you enjoy what you are doing and do it well.

In your new freelancing career _expect to start out slow and consistently grow over time_ because you might have months without having a single client.

Trust is built by admitting mistakes, having patience and being fair with your clients. Treat them as you would like to be treated.

When you want to scale and grow your business, _the easiest way to scale is with a deep client relationship_.

Are you practicing healthy and loving relationships in all areas of your life? _How you act in the rest of your life will be reflected in your work online_.

This last chapter is very important if you want to succeed as a freelancer.

Read on...

Having clients and customers is like dating. You both need to get what you need

Having clients and customers is a lot like dating in the sense that you both need to get what you want if you're going to have a good relationship.

If you're just trying to get something for yourself without consideration for the other person, you're not likely to have a good relationship. Just like dating, you can only handle so many clients and customers at a time, based on who you are.

Now with doing things online, obviously you could handle a lot more customers, more than you can date. The point is you only have a limited capacity to give and you can only give so much. If you just have one client, you can give a lot more to that one client. If you have *100* clients, you can give very little to any of those clients or if you have thousands of customers, you can give very little to any customer that requires your actual time and effort invested in.

The idea is to figure out what it is that you need, and figure out what it is any client or customer with you needs also. The easiest way to do that is just to communicate and listen to feedback, especially with customers. You often get so much good feedback from customers even in the form of negative reviews or complaints.

You can see where you're not meeting needs and that often can guide you into where you are. So if you are looking at it more like dating, and less like business where you just have to go out there and make money, then you'll understand that what you need is the right client and customer for you and you'll be right for them.

I made the mistake a lot with my clients just like I did in dating to focus on only what I wanted. I wanted their money and that's all I wanted. I got their money and I didn't give very much of it though because just like with dating my relentless focus on what I wanted meant that I often completely ignored what they wanted.

Even if they did pay me to do some work, they wouldn't end up paying a lot over a long term because they'd stop working with me. They'd see that I didn't genuinely care about giving them what they needed and so soon enough, they'd stop paying me and I stopped getting what I needed.

I'd be miserable then and desperately looking for another client. That went on and on that way. I started out the same way with my customers once I started having products. I just needed to get these customers to pay me instead of figuring out what it was that they really wanted out of paying me.

What is it you really want out of buying this book or something else? The more you can figure that out, then you can give and focus on the giving.

That's what I do today, I focus on the giving.

What am I giving? What am I doing for someone else?

That is how I've been able to build a great relationship with my wife. What am I doing for her? When you relentlessly focus on what you are doing for the other person, they will often respond by making sure you get what you need also. Your customers make sure they pay you and your clients will make sure they send you your payment in a timely manner.

Your clients will make sure they keep having more work for you and your customers will keep buying more products.

I'm honored to have so many customers buying my courses. I've got feedback from a customer who said: *"Jerry, when I see you have a new course and the title matches anything that I think I might need, I just buy it. I don't read the landing page and I don't watch the promo video, I just buy it because I know you do good work."*

That's what you want to give. When people know that you give, you will get unquestioningly. Clients and customers will just give to you on faith and on trust, the same as a good partner in dating.

When you look at it more like dating where you need a healthy relationship with your clients and customers instead of trying to just make money and exploit them, it will make a world of difference for everything your are doing with them.

Fewer clients that love you is better than a lot of clients that like you

Having a few clients or customers that love you is worth way more than having a lot that don't care that much. If you want to have your full potential fulfilled, then go for deep relationships with a few people especially in the beginning.

The easiest way to scale having clients is not to get more, and believe me I know that from the hard way. I got hundreds and it's miserable to scale a hundred clients. The way I successfully scaled my clients was to do more for less clients, get to know on a surface level a few clients, and get to do really valuable work for the clients that can afford to have me do it.

I have one client who has paid more than all the hundreds of other clients I have had combined. Think about that: *One client has paid more than hundreds of clients combined.* An average client paid several hundred dollars and one client had deeper work I could do. When you build deep relationships with your clients and customers, it's so much easier to scale. Almost all the scaling efforts I see are to get more new people and believe me that's what I did and it was the hard way.

What I do now is aim to build deeper relationships and lots

of my *Udemy* students have taken two to ten other courses with me.

They may have watched a bunch of my *YouTube* videos first, found my website, or heard about me from a few people just like you did before buying this book.

This is proof of the deep relationship value I have now. I made deep relationships as much as I can with as many of my customers as possible. I sit and give thoughtful answers to their questions in my courses.

With clients, it's just like dating again. You can usually get the most out of having one person love you as their number one person in the world than having a bunch of people like you.

In fact, you can get almost nothing out of having a bunch of people like you or think you're hot or cool, but you can get everything out of having one person really love you as their main number one person.

If you think of your clients the same way, you can go places so far beyond that you can ever imagined by being that number one person your client trusts.

Joseph had worked with me for thousands of hours and he

practically works full time with me. Technically, he is a freelancer because he is a contractor who can work wherever and whenever he wants.

Joseph has built a very deep relationship with me where he is trusted to do everything in my business and it is hugely beneficial for both of us. What he has gotten out of it in terms of pay and influence continued to go up and up and up from where it started.

It's just amazing now because it's the same as the relationship I have had with my number one client. *Joseph* continues to do more and more and he is trusted. Aim to be that number one person for the right client knowing that you don't know which client it will be.

I doubt that *Joseph* would have figured that out of all his friends on *Xbox* and in life that building a good relationship with me will be very good for his career. I seriously doubt he would have imagined that at any point prior to it starting to happen.

I had no idea that a client that seemed just like all the other clients would turn out to have so much work that I could do with them. I had no idea because they started out with a small order and it was hard to communicate because English was not their first language.

I did not expect hardly anything and yet built a deeper relationship. I actually flew all the over way across the ocean to their country to meet them. They are the only clients that I've ever had that I actually met.

If you can understand that building deep relationships is usually valuable and you don't know whose worth building a deep relationship with until you have already done it, then you can get amazing returns out of every effort you spend working and presenting yourself online, and doing work for your clients and your customers.

Going from zero to one client is the biggest difference

The biggest difference in clients and customers is going from zero to one just like anything you are likely to do. Having a *YouTube* channel and getting that first video uploaded is the biggest difference. Having your *WordPress* website and getting that very first blog post written is the biggest difference.

In life, zero to one is by far the biggest difference. In pricing for example, going from free to one cent is the largest incremental step. Anything from one cent to two cents almost doesn't make a difference.

When you get your very first client or customer, or you get your very first *YouTube* video uploaded, your very first *WordPress* post done, your first freelancing profile up, your first job invitation on a freelancing website, these are the things to be celebrated.

These are gigantic steps like man's first step on the moon. One small step for man and one giant leap for mankind. It's the same way for you. It might look like one small step to get that video uploaded, but it's a gigantic step for what you are doing.

I often didn't get very excited about taking that first step because I felt like I was so far from what I wanted to do. I felt like one client just emphasized the point that I didn't have ten clients. One customer just emphasized how pathetic it was that I could only make one sale on *Udemy* a year and a half ago when I made my very first sale.

You'd think I would have been so happy about it and I was just frustrated like, *"God, all I can make is just one stupid sale?"*

I got my first *WordPress* post up and you know what I felt?

"Oh man, I got one stupid post up now that's great. Now, I have 99 more to go before I get a decent blog up."

Same thing on *YouTube*, *"Look I got my first video up and no one's watched it, that's great."*

If you can have a positive attitude about taking that first gigantic step, then what you can do is enjoy each step you take instead of taking each step as a means to an end.

You can say: *"Wow, I really feel accomplished, I got that first WordPress post up. That is such a huge difference from having none up, I feel really good! I feel so good I'd probably do another one."*

YouTube is one of the few places that I got so excited. I uploaded my first video, then I uploaded a bunch more videos after it and now I have over five hundreds on my free channel. On my paid channel, I have over three hundreds and will soon have over a thousand when I get all the videos off my computer.

That zero to one is a giant step and the nice thing is that it's usually a step you can take. If you don't have an *Upwork* profile, go to make one. If you don't have a freelancing profile on *Fiverr*, a *WordPress* website or a *YouTube* channel, it's so easy to go take that first step.

Now, doing your first video on *YouTube* will likely take more energy and effort than to do *10* videos well in the future. You won't get to do ten videos if you don't do one. You won't get to ten blog posts when you don't do one. You won't get to ten clients if you don't do one.

So, celebrate!

Whenever you got that one, celebrate it!

Be happy with it!

Aim for it!

You don't need to aim to do a hundred videos or to get a hundred clients like I often did. You aim to get one client and when you've got one client, you aim to get two clients. When you have two you aim to get three.

That's what I do with my sales on *Udemy* now, they're going really well and I aim to do a little bit better each month. I don't need to go straight to some crazy number. If I do a little bit better every month, it will get into a crazy number at the end.

I hope this is useful for you in making sure you celebrate all of the things you do right. It might not seem like much to get your first video, blog post or client, but when you celebrate that big change then you're on your way to having bigger things happen than you ever could have, if you just aim for them to start with.

Forget scaling until you enjoy what you are doing and do it well

I have great news for you. You can forget about scaling until you really enjoy what you are doing. When talking with entrepreneurs and freelancers online, the number one word I think up when it comes to the future is scaling.

"Scaling" is making more money. It's being grandiose, it's having a huge website, it's having all this momentum, energy and excitement.

Forget about that until you love what you are doing and you'll be happy doing it every single day. I've learned this the hard way and you don't have to. I tried to scale all kinds of things I didn't enjoy doing.

Do you know what happened?

I wasted a lot of money and I failed really hard. I nearly went bankrupt and I got to hate my business.

Do you want to do all that or do you want to enjoy what you love and do everyday?

I have a friend I talked with online. I made some courses with him, he does awesome work and he's got tons of skills that are really useful. The main thing he is at right now is the scaling. He won't hardly do anything unless it can be scaled and his challenge is that he consistently is doing things he doesn't like, and that is why he is always trying to do new things.

I'm very lucky because I love doing what I do. This is the best thing you can reach and there's nothing you can hope for that is better than loving what you are doing, and having the chance to do it.

That is way more important than scaling.

Why do you want to scale?

Almost always it sounds something like this:

Well, I want to be able to not work.

I want to be able to do more good.

I want to really help people.

I want to have more money.

I want to have a nicer place to live.

I want to provide for my family.

I want to make an inheritance.

What are all those things? They are things in the future and often in the distant future.

Let's go a little farther into the future:

I really want to have a really nice funeral. Everyone shows up and it's a great party.

In a hundred thousand years, I want to still be remembered and I don't want to be forgotten about with everyone else.

In two billion years, screw it! No one is going to remember me any way. No matter what I do.

That's what the future holds and that's where the future goes. *In two billion years* in the future is just as relevant as *twenty years* in the future or *ten years* because it's not here now.

You have work to do today.

There is a great story I read in some book:

It's about an *American CEO* who is on a trip in *Mexico*. He is trying to explain to a fisherman in *Mexico* about his way of life. The fisherman tells him first that he goes out everyday. He goes fishing and he catches a few fish. Then he comes back in to sell his fish. In the evening he goes out to the tavern, or whatever it is called in *Mexico*, and has a few drinks, dances and has fun with his friends. He then goes home and sleep.

That's what he does every single day.

The *American CEO* asks him: *"Why don't you hire some people to do the fishing for you because then you can go make more money, and you won't have to go out fishing?"*

The *American CEO* continues: *"You could start a franchise out of it and you could get your fishing company all over the world. You can travel and see all these places. Then, in twenty years, you'll have enough money to just retire and set out, go fishing all day and go hang out with your friends later at night at the tavern."*

You can see that what the *American CEO* is trying to work so hard for, is what the *Mexican* fisherman already has everyday.

He already loves what he does everyday and he doesn't need to do anything else. If you love what you're doing, you won't need all of this validation. The quest for scaling is usually a quest for validation. It's an ego trip and it's this desire to build an idea of who you are up into something massive.

If you are pursuing everything you are doing online with the intent to build your definition of you up, it will always disappoint you. The only thing you can do get past that is to find what you love to do and do it.

It's that simple.

I love what I am doing and I would be honored to do it as long as I'm needed for the rest of my life. I would be happy doing it every single day for the rest of my life. It's awesome and that is the magic!

That's the opportunity which is available for freelancing online and yet the easiest way you can screw it up is to focus always on scaling, and to focus always on using now as a means to an end.

This is why I put so many of these motivational sections in this book because when you go into a company it's more obvious that you can't get that far ahead most of the time.

Freelancing online allows all of these illusions and using

things like means to an end. In fact it is much easier to be miserable because you are trying to scale online. I know because I tried to scale everything before, and you know what? All I've got is more misery.

No matter how big it got, I wasn't doing work I enjoyed and I still was miserable. I kept thinking that someday in the future I'll get to the promise land where then I would have big enough scale and everything will be perfect.

No matter how much bigger it got, even to amazing places that I would have never thought of before, I still had the same dissatisfaction.

If you can see that dissatisfaction at the bottom that you are hoping to validate through the future, then you can stop and look for work that you enjoy doing today.

Forget about scaling because when you do work you love, you will scale naturally.

Now, my business is at a larger scale than it has been and yet, all I'm doing is work I love each day. I'm doing work I love and work to support it each day.

That's all I'm doing.

Whatever scale it takes is up to what you need and it's not up to what you ought to have. I hope this has the chance to save you a lot of time, energy and frustration with trying to scale.

Expect to start out slow and consistently grow over time

What expectations do you have right now for growing and getting your business going online?

Are you expecting that you are going to grow pretty quickly and that in a month or two, things will be going really well?

When you start working online you can have expectations that are very challenging. If you start setting all these expectations on what will happen like I did, you'll get frustrated fast.

I had so many expectations that I would consistently be disappointed. I would expect everything to start growing so fast the first year or two I worked online because I had these ridiculous expectations.

I put up a website and I'm looking everyday expecting it's going to rank on search results. I'm expecting that people are going to be visiting it even though I just launched the website a few days before.

I had these crazy expectations that I'll be making a thousand a month in a few months when I just started out online selling all these shirts. My expectations ruined all the celebration of the good things that were happening.

I made a few hundreds selling T-shirts in the first few months and hundreds of people were buying all my designs, which were not even good, and yet I couldn't celebrate it because I expected to make enough money that I wouldn't have to do my existing job. I was disappointed and gave up on it.

Most of the good things that will happen to you will take a lot of consistent time and energy. What you see me doing on *Udemy* is a product of thousands of these videos, hundreds of days in a row of consistently thinking about working on *Udemy*, having an average of five videos I've made everyday before it paid very well!

Most people freelancing online do not get past those first few months of very slow progress. Regardless of where you are, whether starting out or doing this for a while, the lower you can make your expectations, the more you can do.

I know when I made my first thousand in a month on *Udemy*, I was so excited because for once, I had thought: *"This is stupid. It's not going to make any money."*

I had really low expectations for it and after months of disappointment, frustration and expecting nothing, I made *$1,000* one month after making *$99* the previous month.

I was very happy when it went up a little bit the next few months and I was great, but then when it dropped to *$600* a couple of months later I was really disappointed.

Thankfully I kept doing the work in *Udemy* because I love doing it and then that's when things just went nuts. *Udemy* pretty much lost its mind after that and the sales went up an absurd amount. I would have never gone that far with it if I have had these rigid expectations like I had for the whole rest of my business, about how things should be and how far they should go. I would have never got to a thousand a month.

If you want to get higher, having expectations that are low or minimal, or at least being aware of the expectations you do have, will make it a lot easier.

My mom said the only way she could be happy with my dad being married to him is to have no expectations at all because every single thing he did for her then was wonderful and was not taken for granted.

I try and apply the same thing to freelancing and working online and that's the same result I get out of it.

I hope this is useful for you.

Trust is built by admitting mistakes, having patience and being fair

Trust is one of the foundational things you'll want to build when working online in order to go anywhere. You'll need to have trust with your customers and with your clients in order to get their business. When you are working with someone in person it's a bit easier to build trust, even working over the phone. Trust can be very challenging to build when working online because there are so many other people online.

How does someone know that you are any different from any of the other billion plus people that are online? How does someone know that you are trustworthy after they've been scammed several times online? Trust is built most easily by honestly sharing your mistakes.

I don't mean just shotgun sharing every mistake all over the place and getting yourself in prison, I mean honestly sharing your mistakes when it's relevant, appropriate and useful.

That's what people consistently have told me because I share with them when I screw things up, I'll write a post or I'll be honest about it. With my best clients, we've built trust over

Jerry Banfield & Michel Gerard

time by admitting honestly our mistakes.

The fact is that in any relationship you have with anyone, you're going to make mistakes. When you'd honestly admit those mistakes and try to fix them, then you build trust. Trust doesn't come from just everything going great and everything being perfect.

Trust comes when you say, *"Ok, I messed this up, I'm really ashamed of it and it hurts. Let's fix this."* That's what happens in relationships, lots of times the biggest opportunity on having romantic relationships is to grow after you made a mistake, honestly face it and look to move forward.

Yet the challenge is if you're going so fast, you don't even want to look back at those mistakes. If you've been running from your mistakes your whole life, you won't even want to look back and let all the mistakes catch up with you.

I had to stop and start looking at all my mistakes through all of my life before my work online got truly effective. Online, I made tons of mistakes. I had people pay me that I never even delivered service to and they never asked for a refund, so I never gave it to them.

I made all kinds of mistakes like delivering a client's

campaigns wrong. I did a horrible job and wasted the client's ad money. I made all kinds of mistakes working online. I've got suspended and banned from a bunch of different websites. I have had all kinds of painful failures.

I talked about those failures and you can find lots of them on my website and on my *YouTube* channel. I got hit with a *YouTube* copyright strike and it was really painful. *Udemy* said that if I did anything else against the spirit of their policies that they will wipe my account. That hurts a hell of a lot after working almost a year full time on *Udemy*.

I made so many mistakes on *Udemy* that they said: *"Look, stop or we're going to get rid of you."*

I went to them and I said: *"I am sorry. I see what I've done and I've gone against the spirit of all the policies. I exploited loopholes. I've outright broken some rules and I'm sorry. I will do my best everyday to stay within the policies and to be a good useful instructor on your website."*

That is how you build trust.

In my *LinkedIn* profile, it's been the same thing. I had all kinds of issues for my *Facebook* ads. I've got a *Facebook* page stolen after getting it banned from ads.

Honestly face your failures, especially with yourself, and if you want to build trust when you screw something up with a customer, let them know.

When I get a one star review now, I understand that I have screwed a lot of things in my courses and sometimes a one star review will motivate me to fix things. Sometimes, it won't help anyone out. There are people who could have used the course and enjoy it, but they don't because they are scared that it is not worth their time. It's just how things are, you do your best, you admit your mistakes and you keep going.

I know that the main barrier I had getting started online was failure. In *2005*, when I was still in college, I tried to get going online. I got new on *MLM* scheme locally and I tried to do survey things to make money online.

I was so scared of failing that I got my money back from both *MLM* and the surveys. I was so scared of failing that I stopped trying for six more years. If I failed, then I had to cover up all my mistakes and I didn't want to have to do that.

When you are willing to admit your mistakes, you stand a lot too! People love to pitch this big overnight success stories, but if anyone talks to me you'll hear me say that this was no overnight thing. This was no simple and this was a hell of a lot of work all the time consistently for years doing the most good I can everyday and making a ton of painful mistakes.

I had for example a *$8,000* book keeping error with my number one client and this is where our relationship really grew. I noticed it and I didn't say anything for a few days about it because I wasn't sure what to do.

At first I thought, *"Oh my god, I've made this massive mistake and now I owe them 8,000 more dollars."* I already was financially strapped and closed to bankruptcy. I knew the right thing to do was to tell them and I think they actually noticed the error before I did, but they didn't say anything. They waited to see if I would bring it up and when I brought it up, in less than a month, they had a new contract worth around five plus times what the old contract was worth.

I made an honest mistake that I didn't mean to do and it took me months to notice it. Then, when I did, within a month, they trusted me enough to give me five times as bigger of a contract as before. That's a perfect example of how admitting your mistakes, especially when they are relevant in the work you are doing, would allow you to build some deep meaningful relationships.

I have a guy that works with me online and that's what I

like when something goes wrong he'll talk to me about it: *"You know Jerry, I'm sorry I got this account suspended or you know I paid this guy and he didn't give me anything back."* We admit when we screw things up and that's why we have a good relationship.

The easiest way to scale is with a deep client relationship

When you want to scale and grow your business, the easiest way to do it is through deep relationships with the people you already have. What I tried to do most when freelancing online was to find new people all the time. The easiest thing to do is just to build deeper relationships with the people you already know.

When I'm selling my courses, the easiest thing I can do to make sales is to make sure I give value to students who are already the most connected and have the deepest relationship with me.

When I look at my sales, there are students who buy *3* to*10* of my courses and that's where I'm really doing well in sales. Selling to existing students is the easiest way I have to scale. What works the best for me is to provide additional value to the people who've already got value from me.

When you are serving clients, it's much easier to do more for one client than it is to find another client. In fact, the top value client that I'm still working with today, has paid more than working with hundreds of clients combined. Yet, this top client made just a regular order to start with.

We slowly scaled up from a hundred to a few hundreds, then to a thousand to a few thousands, and they eventually gave me a six figures contract. That is possible when you build deep relationships with a few people.

It's completely different from what you see most of the time, where people are trying to always get someone new going. What do you think the lowest cost sales I get with advertising are? The lowest cost sales I get are when I use *Google AdWords* to show ads to people that have already been to my website for *Udemy* courses. Those sales are the easiest I get.

Showing remarketing ads to people who have already looked at and often already bought a course to just tell them that they can buy other courses are the easiest sales that I get on *Udemy*.

The easiest engagement on *Facebook* and in *YouTube* that I get is showing new videos to people who have already watched my other videos. It's a beautiful thing to build deep relationships with people and it's the same as dating.

Most of my life, I thought that if I dated as many girls as

possible that it will work out the best and yet the whole time what I really wanted was a wife. I wanted one girl that we could be both each other's number one with. It was challenging because I thought that going out with more girls was better instead of looking that what I really needed was to build a deep relationship with one.

If you are trying to use *Upwork*, you might need to get five clients to have a good one, but the best way to get more money on *Upwork* is to build deep relationships with every single client you get.

Now, you can't control what the other party gives. All you can do is give the most you have to offer within your limitations, and to follow everything else that I've shared in this chapter in terms of admitting your mistakes, being patient, fair and honest.

When you give what you want to get, you will keep getting better and better and it's amazing. I hope this is useful for you and that you'll have the chance to have an easier time after learning how to be successful freelancing online.

The competition is going up and it is something you can get ahead of using what you have just learned.

How you act in the rest of your life will be reflected in your work online

If you want to have great relationships with your clients and your customers, the key is to practice your relationships consistently across all of your life.

Does this take a lot of effort?

Yes.

Does it have a huge reward?

Yes.

I'm grateful for the kind feedback I've received over and over again in my *Udemy* courses from students. They appreciate that I answer all their questions, they thank me for being a real person and for caring about them.

The only reason I can do that is because I am practicing this in all areas of my life. What you're getting from me is the same thing that my wife, my mom, my friends and family are getting from me.

I am practicing healthy and loving relationships in all areas of my life. I needed a lot of help with this in the past and I need help with it now because I go to a support group everyday. You have to maintain good relationships with all the people in your life.

Before I started taking better care of myself and my relationships in my life, my relationships with clients could never be that good because I would try to be on my best behavior with clients and ultimately would always fail.

One day it would fail and this was easy to see. I'd be playing *Xbox* screaming at people, calling people names and being really mean. I'd be calling my mom up and be giving her a hard time. I'd be calling my brother up and judging him for what he was doing. I'd be really inconsiderate with my wife like staying up late and making a lot of noise.

At some point, I would generally practice that in some way with a client. It would be an inconsiderate way of billing them, or it would be not accepting something they offered.

"Hey, would you do a discount if I do five of these with you instead of one?"

No!

The intolerance I had in all my relationships was practiced with my clients. I've lost more client relationships than I hope you ever will. I lost relationships with hundreds of clients. I've only maintained relationships with a handful and that's how my life went before. My life was slashed and burned relationships.

The best things that happened with clients are deep relationships. If you want deep relationships, you can't just be on your best behavior with your clients because at some point you will trash them and won't trust them. You'll take some kind of selfish or self-centered action that will push them away.

If you are taking care of all your relationships in your life, you'll take care of your clients. You can't control what other people do and if your clients don't want to work with you anymore, you can't control it.

You'll be amazed though about what great relationships you can make with your clients if you practice having healthy relationships in all of your life and where there's nowhere to hide. One day your client will catch you on a bad day and you'll give them the same as you give everyone else in your life.

Today, I'm grateful that even on a bad day, I still am taking loving care of my relationships and to be fair, I don't really have bad days anymore. I have great days and I have good days. When you work on and take good care of yourself, you will automatically take care of your clients, and you won't need to be on that best behavior being a professional.

You can just be yourself with your clients and your customers and everything will go beautifully. I hope this is useful for you as I've shared my experience gaining and losing hundreds of clients painfully.

If you can see what you're doing in all of your relationships in your life from an honest point of view, then you can have the best chance to do great with your clients.

CHAPTER 10

10 freelance websites alternatives

Upwork is certainly the most important freelance website since it changed its name from *Odesk* and had *Elance* join them. It is also the most competitive and if you want a chance to get jobs paid at a rate you want, you might be interested to know what the alternatives are.

1. Freelancer

Freelancer is very similar to *Upwork* and has the same small jobs or larger jobs at fixed price or hourly rate.

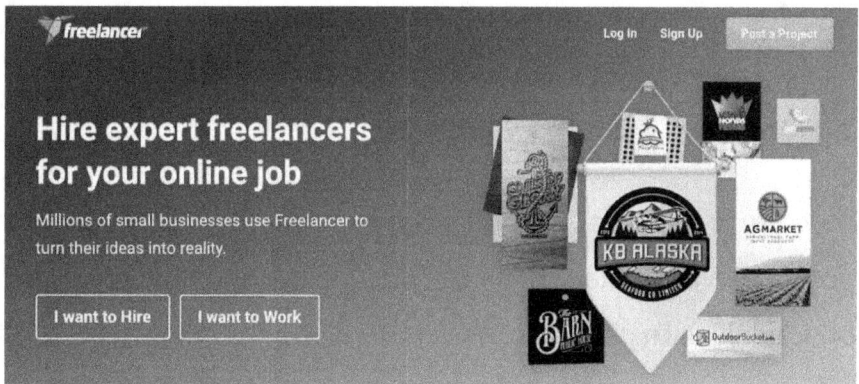

Website: https://www.freelancer.com

2. Toptal

Toptal has a higher hand of developers and designers as their workforce and seems to be very rigorous in their screening process. They write on their website: *"Of the thousands of applications Toptal sees each month, typically fewer than 3% are accepted."*

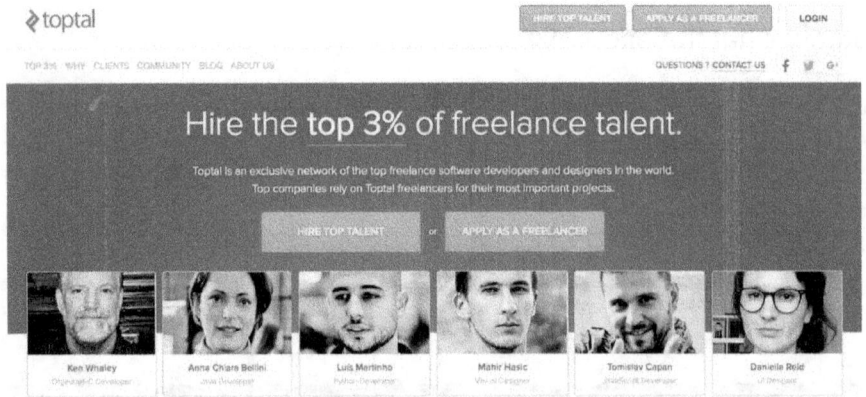

Website: https://www.toptal.com

3. Guru

Guru is a smaller online freelance site and has *5,590* job postings in any category as of today. There certainly are opportunities to get some work from them.

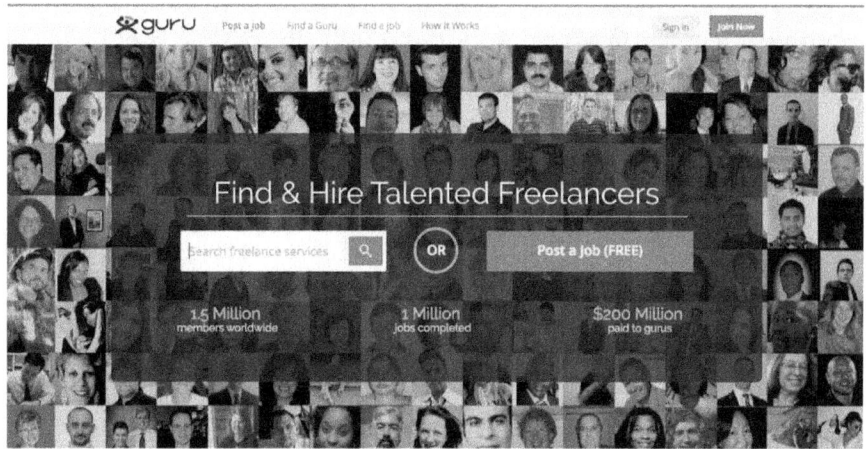

Website: http://www.guru.com

4. Peopleperhour

Peopleperhour is a similar site to *Upwork* with a *Fiverr* touch. You can apply for jobs and also post fixed price offers called *"Hourlies."*

Website: http://www.peopleperhour.com

If you have a fixed price service you do for *$60* for example, you can post it here.

5. 99designs

99designs is for designers and the way it works is that buyers post a contest for which you participate. You may have fifty freelancers providing a design to the client who will choose the one he likes best.

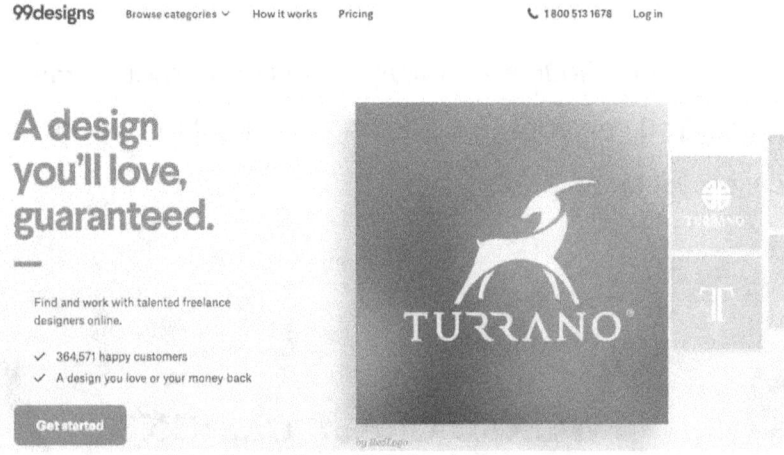

Website: https://99designs.com

6. IFreelance

iFreelance is different from the others because freelancers pay a monthly fee to see offers and bid. The website says, *"Plans start at less than $7 a month!"*

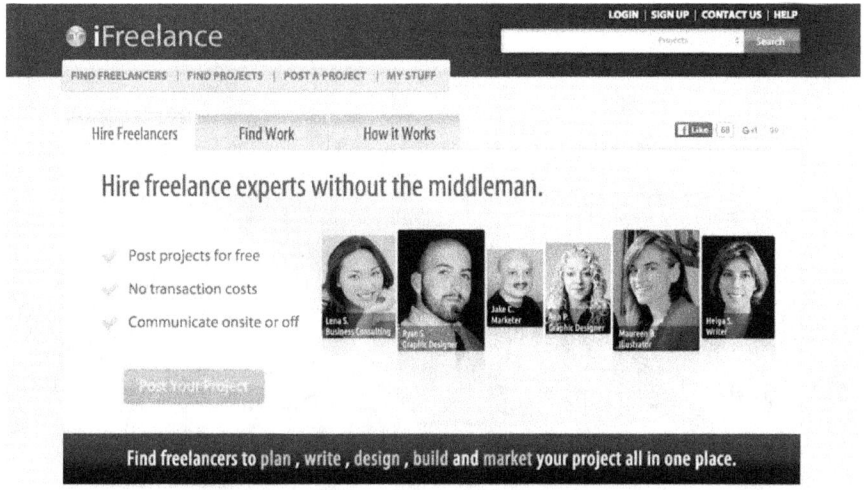

Website: https://www.ifreelance.com

There is no transaction cost and you can communicate with the client off site.

7. Project4hire

Project4hire has all kind of work. There are two options for freelancers, *Basic Freelancer* where you can bid on all jobs, but pay a *$5* fee to accept a project; or *Premium Freelancer* where you pay *$10* monthly and no other fees. Upgrade is possible.

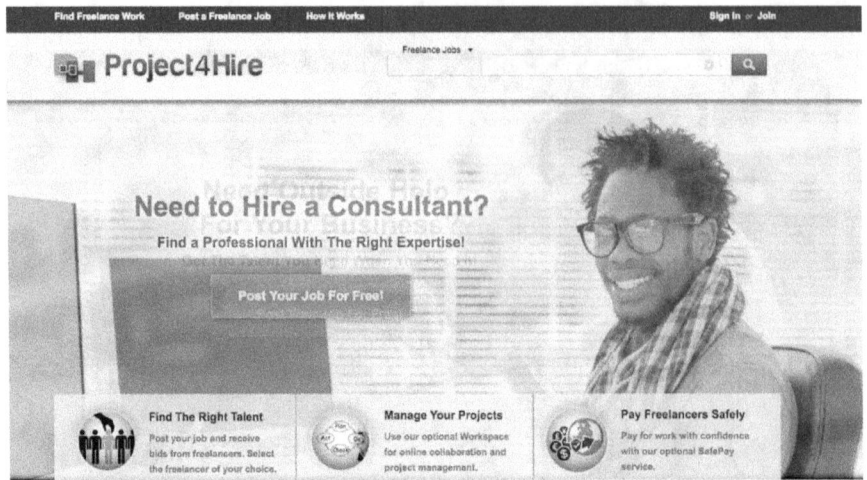

Website: http://project4hire.com

8. In ProFinder

In ProFinder is a program run by the social network *LinkedIn*.

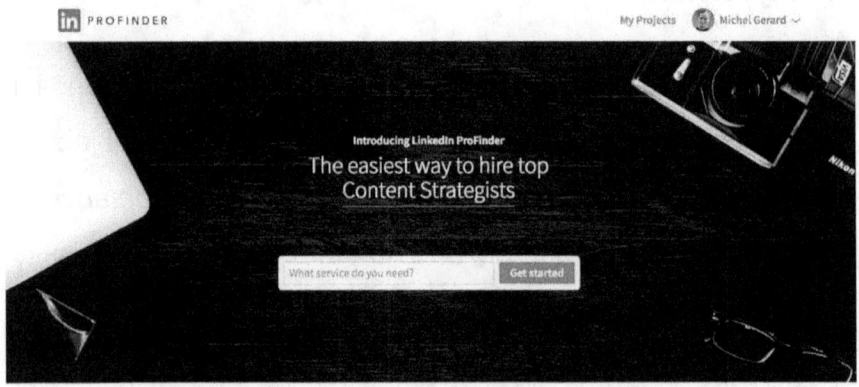

Website: https://www.linkedin.com/profinder

It is directly connected to your *LinkedIn* profile and has jobs in design, writing and editing, legal and software development. It is available only in the *USA* at the moment.

9. CrowdSource

CrowdSource seems different from the others. This is what they say: *"Give your freelance career a boost with a consistent, flexible and reliable source of select assignments from leading enterprises around the world."*

Website: http://www.crowdsource.com

10. FlexJobs

FlexJobs is a job service where you can find part-time and freelance work they call *"Telecommuting"* jobs. They screen all jobs to make sure they are legitimate. There is a low-cost fee ranging from *$14.95* per month to *$49.95* per year.

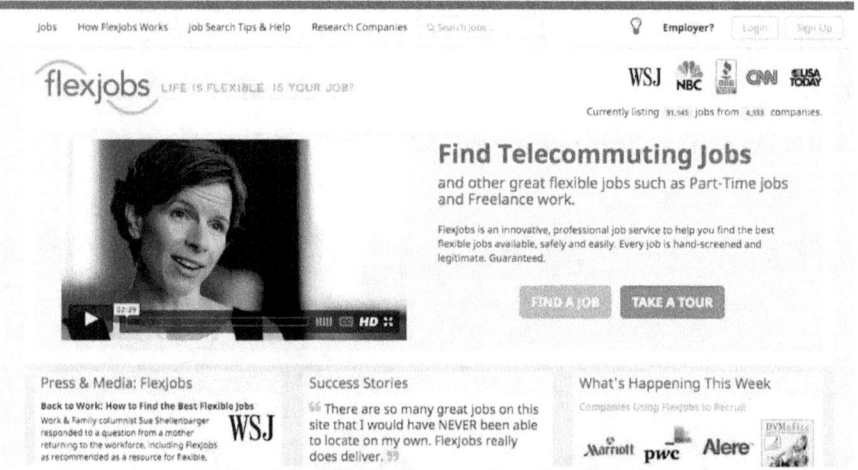

Website: https://www.flexjobs.com

As you can see there are many options available for freelancers to find work online these days. The goal is not to be a member of all sites, but to work with the ones that are best for what you do.

I hope this last chapter is useful to you and I wish you the best of success in finding work online as a freelancer.

CONCLUSION

Thank you for reading this book!

If you want to be successful as a freelancer online, you might also be interested to take my online course *"Freelancing with YouTube, WordPress, Upwork and Fiverr!"* which has served *5,800+* students.

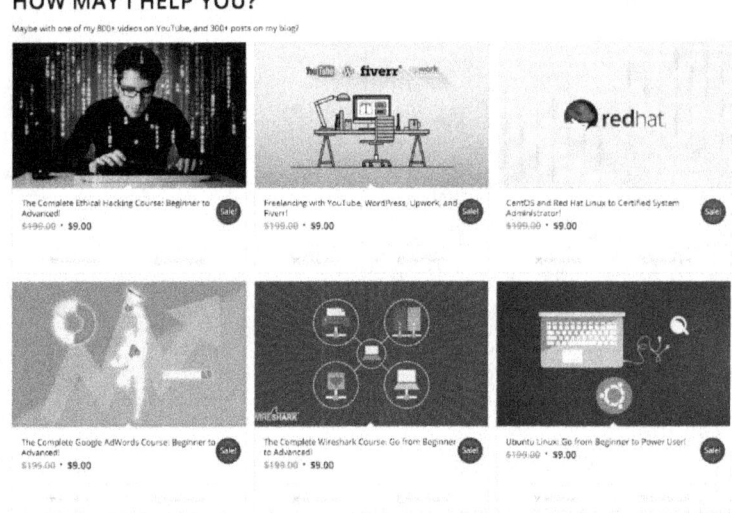

START LEARNING NOW

https://jerrybanfield.com/product/freelancing/

You can read more books written by me at *https://jerrybanfield.com/books*.

I appreciate the time you spent reading this! If it has been helpful for you, I hope you will let others know that in a review at *http://jerry.tips/kindle06jb*

Jerry Banfield

https://jerrybanfield.com

LEGAL NOTICE

The Publisher has strived to be as accurate and complete as possible in the creation of this book, although he does not warrant or represent at any time that the contents within are accurate.

While all attempts have been made to verify information provided in this publication, the Publisher assumes no responsibility for errors, omissions, or contrary interpretation of the subject matter herein. Any perceived slights of specific persons, peoples, or organizations are unintentional.

In practical advice books, like anything else in life, there are no guarantees of results. Readers are cautioned to reply on their own judgment about their individual circumstances to act accordingly.

This book is not intended for use as a source of health, legal, business, accounting or financial advice. All readers are advised to seek services of competent professionals in health, legal, business, accounting and finance fields.

www.ingramcontent.com/pod-product-compliance
Lightning Source LLC
Chambersburg PA
CBHW070228190526
45169CB00001B/119

* 9 7 8 1 5 3 5 0 9 0 2 7 8 *